BOUTIQUE LONDON

A HISTORY: KING'S ROAD TO CARNABY STREET

ENDPAPERS
Mapped out for its readers in
1966, *Rave's* guide to Swinging
London marked boutiques in
pink, restaurants in blue and
nightclubs in green.
Rave/George Newnes Ltd.

Richard Lester

...eet pictured in 1968,
...e of London's earliest
...d still one of the most
...ts in the world.
...n/Rex Features

BOUTIQUE LONDON

A HISTORY: KING'S ROAD TO CARNABY STREET

ACC Editions   *Richard Lester*

© 2010 Richard Lester
World copyright reserved

ISBN 9781851496495

The right of Richard Lester to be identified as author of
this work has been asserted by him in accordance with the
Copyright, Designs and Patents Act 1988. All rights reserved.
No part of this publication may be reproduced, stored in a
retrieval system, or transmitted in any form or by any means
electronic, mechanical, photocopying, recording or otherwise,
without the prior permission of the publishers.

Every effort has been made to secure permission to reproduce
the images contained within this book, and we are grateful to
the individuals and institutions who have assisted in this task.
Any errors are entirely unintentional, and the details should
be addressed to the publisher.

British Library Cataloguing-in-Publication Data.

A catalogue record for this book is available from the
British Library.

Publication designed and typeset by Northbank, Bath.
Printed in the UK by Empress Litho.

Richard Lester trained with Sotheby's in the
early 1990s, having worked for Osborne & Little
and Liberty, and combines writing with running
an online vintage fashion business based in
Sussex. In 2004 he donated a large collection of
designs by John Bates to the Fashion Museum
in Bath and assisted in organising the designer's
retrospective exhibition at the museum in 2006.
He is the author of *John Bates: Fashion Designer*
(2008) and *Photographing Fashion: British Style
in the Sixties* (2009), both of which are published
by ACC Editions.

ACC EDITIONS

ACC Editions
An imprint of the Antique
Collectors' Club Ltd
Sandy Lane, Old Martlesham
Woodbridge, Suffolk, IP12 4SD, UK
T 01394 389950
F 01394 389999
E info@antique-acc.com

ACC Distribution
6 West 18th Street, Suite 4B
New York, NY 10011, USA
T 212 645 1111
F 212 989 3205
E sales@antiquecc.com

www.antiquecollectorsclub.com

CONTENTS

INTROD

Few cities inspire fashion innovation like London. Certainly not the most beautiful, and no longer the richest or even largest capital in the world, for over a decade it proved easily the most creative, innovative and controversial.

No one reason made it so. It was the result of a period of change so important that its effects are still felt today, but those responsible had one thing in common: they were young.

London in 1955 was largely unchanged since the end of the war and both socially and physically it still bore the scars of a period of marked decline from the height of empire. In fashion terms, young in 1955 was 30.

The appearance of Mary Quant's boutique Bazaar when she was 21, and John Stephen's first menswear shop at a similar age, flagged the starting point of an incredible and rapid evolution in everything from where the young shopped for clothes, ate and danced to where they bought their records. It was to be a complete revolution.

UCTION

One:
Setting the Scene
Vince Man's Shop/HIS Clothes/Bazaar

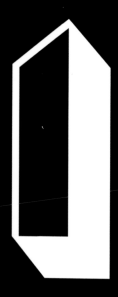

In many ways Carnaby Street mirrored London in its rise to fame in the 1960s; from relative obscurity, it was transformed by the talents of the designers who chose to open there, combined with a healthy dose of luck and timing. Its origins lie almost exclusively in menswear, and in particular the talents of just two people: Bill Green and John Stephen.

Geographically it was well placed, bordering two very different facets of London. To the east the exceptional character of Soho – theatrical, night-based and traditionally the home of London's minority cultures, filled with late night clubs, restaurants and music. To the west the other side of the coin – Mayfair and the department stores of Oxford Street and Regent Street. Between the two, and only a few feet from retail giants such as Liberty and Dickins and Jones, Carnaby Street was cheap, but offered access to both.

The impact that Vince Man's Shop and His Clothes had on the area cannot be underestimated, for they both represented substantial departures from what had gone before. Not just in terms of what they sold, but also in they way they sold it, for the history of Carnaby Street is inextricably linked to the new informality of their boutique retailing.

In a world of menswear essentially unchanged since the 1940s the only real forerunners of both were either traditional menswear chains such as Burton or smaller shops such as Cecil Gee, which offered American style drape suits and the 'Italian look' courtesy of a full-time Roman tailor. Via the nostalgic Edwardian formal dressing which literally brought the 'Teddy' boys to the American-influenced bikers' uniform of white t-shirt, jeans and leather jacket, men's fashion arrived at Carnaby Street in the late 1950s looking for a new direction, which it found with the 'Mods'.

By realising and exploiting this early, John Stephen in particular came to dominate the street, but also managed to adapt to a rapidly changing market. What he and other early boutique owners managed to create was a relatively short lived but intensively creative enclave, the influence of which is still felt in the fashion world today.

The King's Road, by contrast, seemed an unlikely place for fashion to flourish, but like Carnaby Street, fashion emerged as the natural consequence of happy coincidence and the grouping of similar establishments. Unlike Carnaby Street it mirrored the High Street of most large provincial towns, with all the local shops residents of the area needed, plus the usual pubs and cinemas, with the Town Hall and Peter Jones as focal points.

The area had always attracted artists, writers and actors, but money was a key factor, and in the late 1950s retail premises could still be leased or even bought relatively cheaply. It was the land of the pioneer, whether it be at the Royal Court Theatre, where George Devine staged the work of George Osborne, or in the restaurants, cinemas and coffee houses which sprang up to serve increasingly younger customers.

The street was peppered with establishments, which were famous within the various groups which used them, sometimes generally well known, more often not. The Pheasantry Club, Chelsea College of Art, the Classic Cinema and Picasso coffee bar all combined to mean that the King's Road was in fact nothing like an average high street. On closer examination it was something out of the ordinary and a perfect setting for the first boutiques to flourish.

As a general rule, retail rents became cheaper the further the distance from Sloane Square, so it was no coincidence that World's End became host to a cluster of designers over the years. The main disadvantage of the area was its relative isolation in terms of public transport, the nearest tube station being a hike to South Kensington or Sloane Square. Hence the King's Road naturally evolved into London's catwalk, with a cluster of boutiques at one end and Sloane Square at the other. It was one long stage set to walk along or to be viewed from the top of a bus.

Vince Man's Shop

5 Newburgh Street, W1

The menswear revolution had an unlikely hero in Bill Green, who opened Vince Man's Shop in 1954. Already established as a physique photographer of note as Vince Studio, he supplied the increasing number of body-building magazines with tastefully erotic shots of budding British talent from his studio in Manchester Street in the West End. Strict censorship laws imposed regulations on 'nudity, taste and decency', so he began to sell versions of the body-conscious clothes he was using in the studio to an appreciative and cosmopolitan audience. By combining this with the generally more relaxed, informal styles he had seen on the continent, he provided a whole generation with a new way to dress, an alternative to traditional menswear which made no concessions to youth, leisure time or colour.

Interviewed in 1964, he recalled being impressed by the style of the south of France: 'the younger people were wearing black jeans and black shirts and I thought "this has never been seen in Britain, everyone is so busy wearing blue jeans, which they can smuggle in from America." So I got black jeans and black shirts and similar things made in this country and they went like a bomb in those days. And I started designing stuff myself. People said the stuff was so outrageous that it would only appeal and sell to the rather sort of eccentric Chelsea set or theatrical way-out types.'

RIGHT AND OVERLEAF
Vince Man's Shop combined body conscious clothing with effective advertising campaigns in early 1960s bodybuilding and music magazines.

What Vince offered were new clothes – tighter fitting, brighter and in more exotic fabrics than mainstream menswear had known to that date. 'I used materials that had never been used before – lots of velvets and silks, trousers made of bed-ticking, and I was the first with pre-faded denims – and I made everything as colourful and bold as I could.' By simply lowering the waistband so that trousers sat on the hips, he managed to inject sex appeal into an article of everyday clothing, and that was exactly what Vince's customers wanted.

Vince's reputation and client base spread as a wider group of people began to buy his clothes, helped by advertising campaigns in body-building, film and music magazines and a comprehensive mail order catalogue. Sean Connery was even recruited in his pre-Bond era as male model to promote Matelot vests at 29/6 each.

By modern standards many of Vince's innovations seem commonplace: tightly fitted t-shirts designed to emphasis the torso or boldly striped bathing shorts, but his ability to combine the risqué with a shrewd business sense laid the foundations for menswear boutiques to thrive over the following decade. It was also no coincidence that he employed a certain John Stephen, who went on to become the undisputed 'King of Carnaby Street', as a shop assistant.

'The only shop where they take your inside leg every time you buy a tie.'

George Melly, *Revolt into Style: The Pop Arts in Britain*, 1970

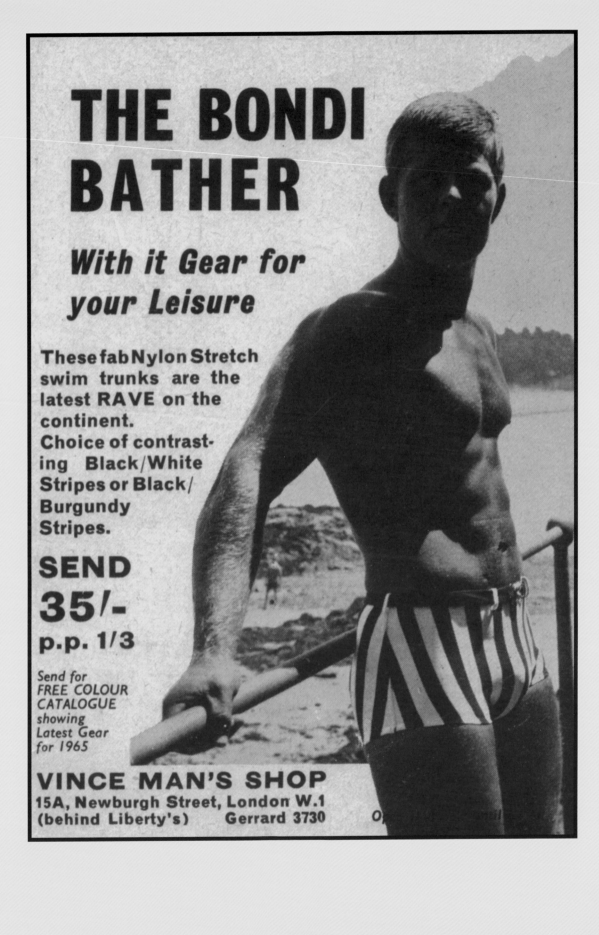

THE BONDI BATHER

With it Gear for your Leisure

These fab Nylon Stretch swim trunks are the latest RAVE on the continent. Choice of contrasting Black/White Stripes or Black/Burgundy Stripes.

SEND 35/-
p.p. 1/3

Send for FREE COLOUR CATALOGUE showing Latest Gear for 1965

VINCE MAN'S SHOP
15A, Newburgh Street, London W.1
(behind Liberty's)   Gerrard 3730

HIS Clothes

5 Carnaby Street, W1

John Stephen's move into retailing was a natural progression from working at Vince Man's Shop, but the way in which he did it could only be put down to his talent for showmanship and his acute understanding of the marketplace.

He arrived in London from Glasgow in 1952 and via Moss Bros and Vince's he launched a stellar career from his first shop in Beak Street in 1957. The opening of HIS Clothes a few months later at 5 Carnaby Street marked the true beginning of the transformation of the street, from run-down obscurity to its brief tenure as an international fashion Mecca.

Being the same age as the majority of his clients, he realised that an increasingly solvent youth market was emerging that wanted to look different, with its own set of rules. These were the 'Mods', whose smart appearance fell somewhere between modern bespoke tailoring and the body conscious clothing sold at Vince's. Youth and music were the key and for the next decade the street thronged with fashion conscious men who relied on John Stephen for their finery.

Interviewed by the US title *Toledo Blade* in August 1965 he commented: 'Young men wanted to wear these clothes and they had the money to buy them, but no-one seemed to want to make the clothes for them. That's when I stepped in. I took a small room in Soho, bought some fabrics I had faith in, hired a sewing machine, got a machinist, designed some clothes and well – I was away.'

He took what had seemed theatrical and daring and made it mainstream, designing and manufacturing at the back of the boutique to keep costs trimmed to a minimum. At the same time he exploited the potential of the central West End location of the street to provide ever-changing window displays to attract customers. The list of John Stephen firsts is substantial: he employed designers of his own age to ensure that every rapid and subtle change in fashion was catered for, his shop assistants were the same age as the clients, and the boutique played the latest music, non-stop.

OPPOSITE PAGE
John Stephen outside one of his many boutiques circa 1963, the undisputed 'King of Carnaby Street'.
Fashion Museum, Bath

OPPOSITE PAGE
Double breasted 'bum-freezer' jackets were a hit in the early 1960s and stocked in the growing number of men's boutiques in and around Carnaby Street.
Rex Features

HIS Clothes became the menswear boutique that was copied across London, eventually across the country, and its style reflected the desire of its clients – to look ultra-sharp at all times. It started with 'Italian' suits based on the continental cut with sharp, thin lapels, teaming them with narrow ties and shoes, then 'bum freezer' jackets (ideal for riding Vespas), then brightly coloured shirts, exotic fabrics and vivid printed ties.

Tall, distinguished and with an Alsatian called Prince, John Stephen was the personification of the lifestyle he was selling. Dubbed the 'King of Carnaby Street' by the press, he frequently featured in articles detailing the trappings of his luxurious lifestyle and, in another first, he became almost as famous as the pop stars buying his clothes.

'Every time you walked past a John Stephen window there was something new and loud in it.'

Nik Cohen, *Today there are no Gentleman*, 1971

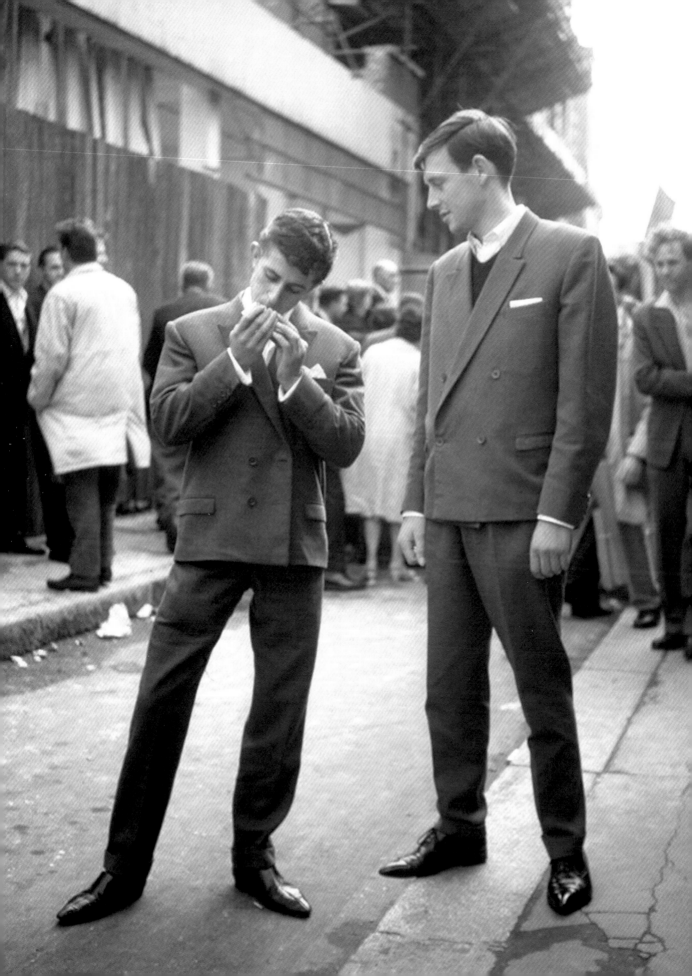

The first boutique of the John Stephen empire, HIS Clothes opened in the late 1950s and was to become the retail model for competitors all over London. *ITV/Rex Features*

TEPHEN
OF LONDON

Two of John Stephen's earliest fans,
Mick Jagger and Keith Richards shop
on Carnaby Street in 1964.
Daily Mail

Bazaar

138a King's Road, sw3
46 Brompton Road, sw3

Mary Quant's journey from designing and making clothes in her bed-sit off the King's Road to becoming a household name epitomised the changes happening in London in the late 1950s and early 1960s. Her boutique was Bazaar and from the heart of Chelsea she managed a one-woman revolution in clothing, marketing and retail design, pioneering the idea of the boutique owner as designer, which was to become central to the evolution of London as the new fashion capital of the world.

She had met her future husband Alexander Plunkett Greene whilst studying illustration at Goldsmiths, she living in Oakley Street, he in a large house just off the King's Road. After investigating a number of alternative business ventures they, along with business partner Archie McNair, put together enough money to buy 138a King's Road to open as a boutique, with Alexander's restaurant in the basement. All three were central to what the press came to dub the 'Chelsea set', a very traditional generalisation which came to represent a group of creative, dynamic and, above all, young residents of an area already renowned for its association with artists. McNair owned the Fantasie coffee bar at 128 King's Road and ran photographic studios above, meaning that a constant flow of colourful characters visited the King's Road. In *Quant on Quant*, published in 1966, she recalled: 'Our friends and acquaintances were painters, photographers, architects, writers, socialites, actors, con-men, and superior tarts.'

Bazaar started by stocking clothes that Quant would choose to wear herself, buying from art college students, jewellers, milliners, creating a hand-picked vision of a new way of dressing which moved away from the idea that one of clothing's primary functions was to be an indicator of social status. When supplies of stock started to dwindle, largely due the success she had at selling, Quant used her bed-sit in Oakley Street as a design studio and workroom to provide her own designs for the boutique. As a novice in the ready-to-wear market she bought fabric at retail prices from Harrods to use with adapted Butterick patterns. Rapid success brought with it the continued problem of stock control and as designs sold in the shop, she and friends would work overnight to replace them the next morning. 'Although at the start we made every mistake anybody could, the need was so strong that we couldn't fail', she told *Design Journal* in 1966.

The Mary Quant look of the late 1950s and early 1960s was one of simple shapes in cotton gabardine, poplin and gingham injecting a youthful informality into clothes which were still

OPPOSITE PAGE
Mary Quant and Alexander Plunkett Green photographed at the newly opened branch of Bazaar in Knightsbridge, 1964. *Hatami/Rex Features*

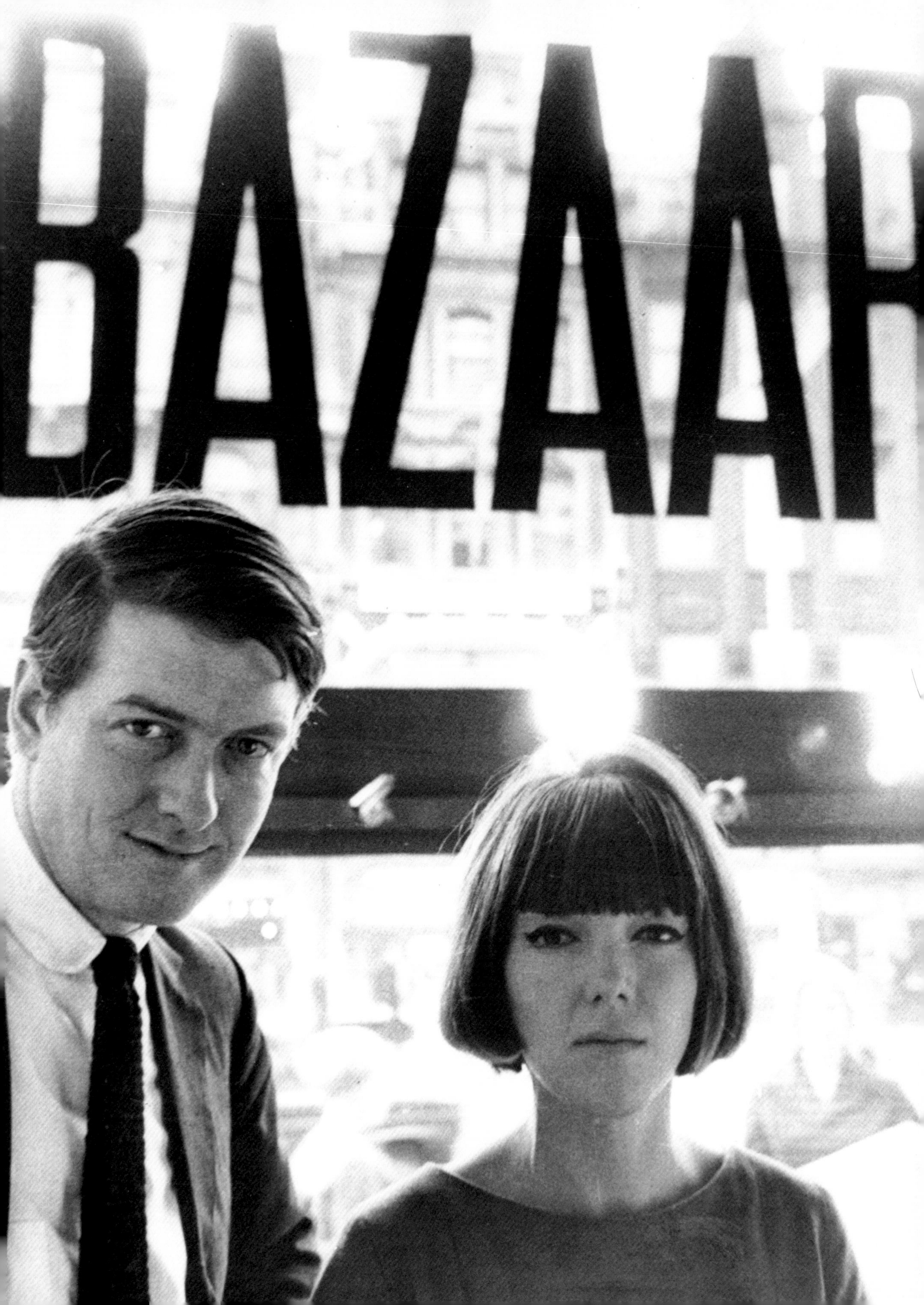
BAZAAR

OPPOSITE PAGE
Jean Shrimpton models Mary Quant,
1964.
John French/Fashion Museum, Bath

OVERLEAF
Window displays at Bazaar aimed
to surprise with their informality
and humour, Knightsbridge 1964.
Hatami/Rex Features

aimed at a relatively wealthy customer. At first the interior of the shop owed far more to the traditional fashion salon than to the cavalcade of brightly coloured boutiques which were to invade Chelsea over the next decade. The difference with Bazaar was the direct link between design, production and sales – for the first time all three became one.

She achieved a sleek combination of tradition and modernity, and of retail and social space which appealed to a wide range of clients, the avant-garde window displays soon becoming an event in themselves. This was the recipe of the boutique which could be adapted and refined to cater for the style of the moment, but the essential ingredients would remain the same for the following 20 years.

Quant's ideas went beyond a single shop and by 1957 she had opened a second branch in Knightsbridge and established Mary Quant Ltd., with headquarters in Ives Street mid-way between the two branches. With her thoughts focused firmly on wholesale ready-to-wear, trips to the US paid off when American retail giant JC Penney placed an order for over 6,000 garments, spring-boarding her from boutique owner to international fashion retailer almost overnight.

In 1962 came Ginger Group, a label solely for wholesale ready-to-wear which enabled Quant's designs to be sold country-wide in fashionable stores and created a larger following for its increasingly youthful styles. The clothes had an almost childlike simplicity – smocks and shifts in linen and crepe, contrasting collars and cuffs, eye-catching trim. The key was shape, with function winning over form, the angular tailoring well suited to the angular hair cut by Vidal Sassoon which was to become a Mary Quant trademark.

Hemlines rose, above the knee in 1964, and by the time the rest of London was awakening to the idea of boutiques, Mary Quant already had two in London, an international wholesale business, and commuted to America once a month.

'Mary Quant opened the door to a new freedom for the young.'

Ernestine Carter, *Tongue in Chic*, 1974

Kiki Byrne
136 Kings Road, sw3

A former employee of Mary Quant, Kiki Byrne was an experienced womenswear and costume designer for theatre by the time she opened her own boutique on the King's Road in the early 1960s. The shop, having almost adjacent windows, is often cited in contemporary accounts as being the closest competitor to Bazaar, with buyers naturally comparing the two.

Donis
23 Carnaby Street, w1

One of Carnaby Street's earliest menswear boutiques, owned and run by Andrew Spyropoulus, it opened in 1957. Donis had the advantage of factory premises in the same street, making slacks in tweeds, mohairs at an average price of 4 guineas, colourful shirts at 49s 6d and being able to complete lightning-fast alterations to customers' purchases.

John Michael
170 King's Road, sw3 and branches

John Michael Ingram had a background in women's fashion before opening a small men's boutique on the King's Road in 1958, eventually expanding the chain to 17 branches in London. Under the John Michael brand he competed in the quality middle market, employing designers such as Gerald McCann to create his modernist shop interiors. At the other end of the scale, his reasonably priced GUY boutiques appealed to younger customers who thronged Carnaby Street and the King's Road every Saturday.

MORE SHOPS

Paul's Boutique
47 Carnaby Street, w1

An up-to-date menswear boutique following the John Stephen lead, owned by Nathan and Susie Spiegal and opened 1959, with a second branch on the street by the late 1960s. A particular favourite with buyers of shirts, with a plethora of designs and colours, prices in the mid-1960s noted as from 49s 11d to 4 guineas.

Mary Fair
18 Baker Street, w1

A traditionally smart women's wear boutique owned by Suzanne Peet and popular in the late 1950s and early 1960s. Renowned for carrying clothes from young designers for day and evening wear.

Two:
New Ideas
Foale and Tuffin/Top Gear/Countdown/
Biba/Clobber

In the first half of the decade the new boutique owners were characterised by a pioneering spirit, but many had also shared art college educations and had fallen into boutique ownership as the natural consequence of a desire to express their own taste in fashion, whether it be as retailers, designers or both. Under the tutelage of Janey Ironside, a disproportionate number had attended the Royal College, with Central St Martin's fashion course also becoming increasingly important.

Their success mirrored a new generation of journalists, photographers, store buyers and models, all of whom acted as effective publicity for their designs. Influential commentators such as Marit Allen at *Vogue* meant that clothes by a younger generation began to appear in magazines that had real national and international importance – at first Mary Quant, then less well-known names, as both their number and influence increased.

Queen magazine was particularly adept at spotting talent early, as were the new titles aimed at younger readers. Molly Parkin at *Nova*, Janet Street-Porter at *Petticoat* (subtitled 'For the Young and Fancy Free') and *Rave*, all had extensive commentary on the latest styles and, most importantly, produced guides to where they could be bought.

Equally important were inspired store buyers like Vanessa Denza at Woollands 21, who proved the catalyst for the success of more than one major designer by placing orders with budding talent in large quantities.

It is perhaps significant that the early players also turned out to be amongst the most important, both in terms in the quality of their contribution to fashion history and also in the length of time their boutiques survived.

Foale and Tuffin

1 Marlborough Court, W1

Marion Foale and Sally Tuffin formed a unique and dynamic partnership and it is generally accepted that had the pair not set up just off Carnaby Street in 1963, the immediate area would have had a very different future. Walthamstow School of Art and then the Royal College of Art introduced them to the legendary Janey Ironside, and both graduated finding they wanted to design and manufacture clothes for modern, active women and to challenge preconceptions about dress, which they saw as restrictive and outdated.

For Foale and Tuffin, the process of achieving an internationally acclaimed business followed a similar course to that of many other designers aiming to set up in a male-dominated fashion industry in the early 1960s. However, the strength and modernity of their designs meant that, even though they were made in their South Kensington flat, influential buyers such as Vanessa Denza at Woollands 21 soon became interested. As orders increased, so did the need for efficient manufacture, but many wholesale fabric suppliers still found doing business with women unusual, often forcing them to buy fabric at retail prices from stores like Liberty in order to complete orders.

With outworkers beginning to be used to make up their clothes, a fellow Royal College of Art graduate and friend, James Wedge, suggested the area around his offices in Ganton Street as a cheap and central location for a workroom and studio. Paying 6 guineas a week, Foale and Tuffin moved their operation to Marlborough Court, a small alley running north of Carnaby Street, with the idea of a boutique evolving from the interest the studio generated from passers-by. They finally opened for business in 1963, becoming the first women's boutique in what was to become a stampede to Carnaby Street over the remainder of the decade

Their clothes were as distinctive as their new white and bright showroom, the shop front peppered with light bulbs and totally unlike traditional fashion shops. They sold hats by James Wedge, handbags by Sally Jess, their mini dresses were short and chic, and included the renowned 'double D' design of 1966, the letters in bright pop-art contrast linen. Trouser suits for women, innovative combinations of Liberty prints and above all a sense of youthful fun were copyrighted Foale and Tuffin.

OPPOSITE PAGE
Marion Foale (left) and Sally Tuffin (centre) with an early design for daywear photographed for *The Sunday Times*, 1961.
Norman Eales/Fashion Museum, Bath

OPPOSITE PAGE
Joanna Lumley models a boldly striped
wool crepe dress by Foale and Tuffin,
1965.
David Montgomery/National Magazines

'Ever since Foale got together with
Tuffin, there's been a definite move
for girls to link their arms and make
their way together in the design
world. Going it alone is becoming
unfashionable.'

Sylvia Hammon, *The Times*, 1966

Top Gear
Countdown
135a & 137 King's Road, sw3

Encouraged by the success of Mary Quant's Bazaar, James Wedge and his partner Pat Booth spotted a shop at 135a King's Road and decided to open Top Gear by 1964. It was to become one of the most celebrated boutiques of the decade, partly as a result of the distinctive stock and retail design elements which attracted attention and emulation, but also as a consequence of the cavalcade of models, actors and rock stars who used the tiny shop as a springboard for the wider King's Road boutique scene.

James Wedge had excelled in hat design and, like Foale and Tuffin, followed a path from art college and was influenced by inspired teaching from the likes of Janey Ironside. On graduating, his designs attracted the attention of couturier Ronald Patterson, and by 1962 he was established on the top two floors of 4 Ganton Street, designing for Patterson but also showing, selling and manufacturing his own designs; the location effectively became his own salon boutique for hats.

In his role as buyer he stocked Top Gear with the very best of modern design available: clothes by Foale and Tuffin, Moya Bowler shoes, handbags by Sally Jess, Janice Peskett belts, his own design hats and simple, modern shift dresses, many produced in tiny numbers by local makers who brought stock in as they finished it. Marry Farrin knitted James Wedge designed cat-suits, photographed for *Queen* by Eric Swayne in Autumn 1965 – a riot of stripes with matching muffler and crochet beret.

Turnover was soon achieving an enormous £1,000 a week and the adjacent Countdown was opened shortly afterwards to expand the amount of useable space; sales were up until then restricted by how many people could physically fit into the modest shop at 135a.

Interestingly, youth magazines such as *Rave* recommended that readers visit Top Gear and Countdown, even though the prices were well above what the average teenager could afford. Such was the impact of these first boutiques, however, that cheaper copies of their clothes were usually available via ready-to-wear wholesalers within weeks of arriving in stock, as were sewing patterns for home-made copies.

OPPOSITE PAGE
Top Gear was described by *Queen* magazine as 'a shop the size of a telephone box', pictured in 1967.
Brian Moody/Rex Features

'A shop the size of a telephone box.'

Queen magazine, 1965

Bringing craft to the King's Road:
rust-coloured wool mini dress by
James Wedge and hand knitted for
Top Gear by Mary Farrin, shoes
by Moya Bowler, 1965.
Eric Swayne/National Magazines

OPPOSITE PAGE
Knitted mini dress and matching hat
by James Wedge for Top Gear, 1965.
Caroline Smith/National Magazines

The King's Road in 1965, soon to become as popular a tourist destination as the Tower of London. *Topfoto*

Biba

87 Abingdon Road, w8
19-21 Kensington Church Street, w8

Biba's postal boutique opened for business in 1963 and any doubts Barbara Hulanicki may have had about the commercial viability of her designs were allayed in 1964, when her simple gingham shift dress appeared in the *Daily Mail* and Biba received 17,000 orders. However, like many of her contemporaries, the logistics of manufacturing larger quantities of clothes presented the immediate problems of sourcing and buying fabric, arranging outworkers, maintaining quality control and arranging delivery.

With a background in fashion illustration, and supported by her husband, Stephen Fitz-Simon, her first Biba designs were simple shapes, practical and fresh. However, whilst other designers continued to develop the angular modernism so often associated with the early boutiques, Barbara Hulanicki began to experiment with the nostalgic Art Nouveau and Art Deco themes that were to become her signature. By reinterpreting design references and making them commercially attractive, her first boutique in Abingdon Road opened in 1964 with the retail environment completely in tune with the clothes it sold. Formerly a chemist's shop, the overriding feeling was of the late 19th century, with the original shop front and fittings adapted for its new use. Biba created a rich and exotic interior in which fantasy merged with fashion, eschewing the contemporary studio for the dark, rich and exotic interiors of the past.

The clothes and shapes were simple, affordable, exotic, using a palette of gold, rich purples and moss greens and accessorised with feather boas, felt hats and printed silk scarves. In its pricing structure Biba deliberately aimed to sell clothes to the shop girls, students and secretaries who realised that what it sometimes lacked in quality, it more than made up for in style.

When Cathy McGowan began to wear Biba dresses to present *Ready Steady Go*, fans watching the show on Friday night realised they could be wearing the same dress as their heroine by the following Saturday and queues began to form in Abingdon Road, a precursor to the move to larger premises in Kensington Church Street in 1966. At the same time the shop attracted actresses, pop stars and imitators, together with acres of press coverage and editorial comment that reaffirmed that Biba had got the formula right, creating a boutique democracy well ahead of its time.

OPPOSITE PAGE
Biba's first boutique on Abingdon Road, converted from a Victorian chemist's shop. The interior was dark and full of richly coloured, affordable clothes, feather boas, bentwood hat stands and potted palms.
David Graves/Rex Features

OPPOSITE PAGE
The ultimate in coordination; matching
mini dress, hat and bag by Biba, 1967.
Peter Atherton/Fashion Museum, Bath

'A shop is fantastic for a designer
because you get an immediate
reaction. You don't have all the
intermediaries; the buyers coming
in and the accountants. It's direct:
if someone likes something they
buy it, and you see it happen.'

Barbara Hulanicki interviewed by the Design Museum, 2007

Clobber

11 Blackheath Village, SE3

Clobber existed as if to prove that the first boutiques opening in central London did not have exclusive rights on popularity. The brainchild of Jeff Banks, it opened in 1964 selling a mixture of original designs by London's newest fashion stars, and was so popular that the stock sold out within a day. As a direct result of not being able to replace it quickly, Banks went into design and manufacture; with a small production team on site, he landed himself in the owner/designer/retailer role which was to prove so successful over the following decade.

All the more remarkable was Banks' rise to the forefront of fashion retailing at 21. After running a paraffin tanker at 13, selling his first business for a profit at 15 and training in art and textiles at Camberwell and Saint Martin's, he made a determined if slightly unusual boutique owner. Combined with an obvious talent for business came a natural eye for style, and like Biba he brought together a myriad of historical references in the design of both the clothes and the shop, including the use of antique furniture to display clothing (not unusual now but in 1964 he was amongst the first).

Married to Sandie Shaw, his designs attracted huge interest and the Clobber label was soon sold in fashionable boutiques throughout London and the UK, including ultra-smart establishments like Stop the Shop and Just Looking on the King's Road, as well as the brand new Top Shop at Peter Robinson.

The golden age for the Clobber brand came later in the decade when he successfully negotiated extensive concessions in US department stores, putting his level of exports on a par with the major UK fashion houses. He excelled at the maxi line and in the use of nostalgic prints, eventually adding the Clobber 2 brand and a Jeff Banks boutique in Mayfair to his empire.

OPPOSITE PAGE
White 'play suit' with buckled belt, shoes by Moya Bowler, photographed against the original Victorian shop window at Biba, 1965.
Marc Hispard/National Magazines

'By the time I was 13, I had a tanker on the road; at 15, I sold the business and saved the money so, by 21, I had the money for a shop. My father mortgaged the family home to get the rest.'

Jeff Banks interviewed by Caitlin Davies for *The Independent*, 2007

Jeff Banks opened Clobber in Blackheath
in 1965 with immediate success, pictured
here at home with Sandie Shaw in 1967.
Topfoto

Anello & Davide
33 Oxford Street, W1

The preferred cobbler to a host of London's designers, famous for popularising the Chelsea boot and for their low heeled mod styles, designed to be worn with the shortest of mini dresses, prices in 1966 ranged from 4 to 12 guineas.

Tony Armstrong
109 Walton Street, SW3

One of the small group of boutique owner/designers selling dresses, suits and coats, with hats by James Wedge and bags by Sally Jess. The shop had huge glass windows, an exposed wooden floor and was a favourite of the *Sunday Times* fashion writers.

Palisades
26 Ganton Street, London W1

Owned by Pauline Fordham, Clive Goodwin and Michael White and renowned for having a juke box and a 'What the Butler Saw' machine as part of the décor by Derek Boshier, customers included 'film and theatrical people', with Janet Street-Porter amongst its early employees.

The interior of Pauline Fordham's Palisades boutique on Ganton Street, complete with 'What the Butler Saw' machine, 1966.
Press Association

MORE SHOPS

Victoria and Albert
28/29 Victoria Grove, w8

Victoria was for the girls, Albert for the boys, stocking a range of contemporary designers behind an original Victorian shop front, described in *Queen* magazine in 1965 as aimed at 'anyone with fashion sense in the 18/30 range'.

You and I
2 Crawford Street, w1

A deluxe boutique owned by Judith Maisel, specialising in complete outfits, dresses, trouser suits, coats, hats and 'cocktail' wear in the 5 to 50 guinea range. Inside, the ceiling was decorated with tented gingham fabric, while the exterior of the shop was guarded by a ceramic greyhound.

Three:
All Dressed Up

*Hung on You/Granny Takes a Trip/
I Was Lord Kitchener's Valet/
Apple Boutique/Dandie Fashions*

By the time Michael Rainey opened Hung on You in 1965, a select and influential group of socialites, pop stars, tailors and fashion designers had begun to gravitate to boutique ownership, some to World's End and the King's Road where Mary Quant had opened Bazaar ten years earlier, others to Portobello Road and further afield.

Together they created a 'network of cool' which was to sustain a group of boutiques destined to become tourist attractions, such was the novelty of their appearance and merchandise. They were united by their brilliance but also, too often, by erratic service, varying levels of commitment and poorly made stock.

With names like Granny Takes a Trip and I was Lord Kitchener's Valet, they subverted the rules of retailing as they saw them, mixing Victorian clothing, military uniforms and ephemera with modern design, psychedelic imagery and Art Nouveau.

It was London's brightest and most temporary boutique revolution, as if a huge dressing-up box was forced open and sold throughout London to a soundtrack of the latest pop hits.

Hung on You

22 Cale Street, sw3
430 King's Road, sw3

As the first of a small group of retailers which have come to symbolise the 1960s boutique movement in popular culture, Hung on You occupies a particularly important place in fashion history. Its customers were the real departure from the routine, for they were almost exclusively the new male dandies invented by the 1960s, a taboo-breaking mixture of social and rock aristocracy as never encountered before. Equally distinctively, and unlike many menswear boutiques that had opened earlier in the decade, it combined references to Edwardian and Regency dress in its clothes, reinventing them with brightly coloured and exotic fabrics and finely tailored jackets.

Hung on You first appeared in 1965, owned by aristocrat Michael Rainey, with the boutique's early incarnation in Cale Street, close to Chelsea Green, moving to 430 King's Road in 1967. Like the many competitors that followed in its wake, the design of the boutique was just as important as the stock. Inverting the principle that a shop front existed for the interior and goods to be seen from the street, Hung on You painted theirs over, creating the ultimate salon to which anyone admitted felt in awe.

Inevitably its particular look, and Michael Rainey's marriage to the socialite Jane Ormsby Gore, meant considerable coverage in the papers for this was essentially an exclusive boutique, built around the idea of the shop as a social hub in the same way as Top Gear and Countdown, but with a very different, less commercially minded approach. As Rainey employed artists Michael English and Nigel Waymouth, collectively known as Hapdash and the Coloured Coat, to design their posters, psychedelic album cover merged with art nouveau and Indian motifs to created a hybrid reflected in the clothes and interior of the boutique and one wall was painted with an enormous mural in the style of Aubrey Beardsley.

Many commentators, Jane Ormsby Gore among them, have since cited the move from Cale Street to the King's Road as the downfall of Hung on You, suggesting that the change of scale and location were enough to destroy the fragile equilibrium of a successful boutique, a story which was to become all too familiar as, in a rush to expand, the individuality and containable overheads of smaller shops were lost.

OPPOSITE PAGE
Hung on You was the first of a new generation of boutiques in Chelsea, opening at 22 Cale Street in 1965.
Getty Images

The return of the dandy – style guru Christopher Gibbs and boutique owner Michael Rainey pictured in 1966.
Colin Jones/Topfoto

'It was just Michael Rainey's colour sense and his choosing this pot of paint rather than that and putting it up. But nobody had the money to change the shell of the building. If there was a hideous staircase going down to the downstairs showroom it stayed, and each bannister was painted a different colour.'

David Mlinaric on the interior of Hung on You, interviewed by the *V&A* in 2006

Outside Hung On You at 430 King's Road, a kaleidoscope of historical and ethnic influences in men's fashion, circa 1967.
Rex Features

Amongst the velvet, beads and vintage
uniforms of the new boutiques the strict
division between male and female dress
codes dispersed.
Malcolm English

Granny Takes a Trip

488 King's Road, sw3

Perhaps the most visually distinctive of all the World's End boutiques was Granny Takes a Trip, owned by Sheila Cohen and Nigel Waymouth, joined by distinguished tailor John Pearse.

Firmly rooted in the traditions of showmanship, the boutique initially opened in 1966 as a way of selling a large collection of antique clothing garnered from London's street markets. When the majority of the stock sold out on the first Saturday, John Pearse went about making replacements, adapting and refining details, creating a distinctive World's End look which was to disseminate into boutique retailing well into the next decade.

'It's a romantic dream world we're catering for', said Nigel Waymouth of his stock. It was a mixture of new and old, men's and women's clothes creating one of London's first all-inclusive boutiques with communal changing rooms. Pearce adapted William Morris furnishing fabrics and used them for tailoring, adjusted the cut or trim of Victorian inspired high-necked blouses adding contemporary touches like elongated collars, effortlessly setting them apart from the originals.

The synthesis between clothes, music and design was personified by the boutique itself, an ever-changing visual feast both inside and out. It began with a giant portrait of Native American Chief Low Dog replaced by one of Chief Kicking Bear, covering the whole of the shop front, and by 1967 it had changed to the Art Deco face of Jean Harlow, and at one stage it sported the variously painted front of a 1948 Dodge car. Boundaries were being pushed, but with humour and irony. The interior was a stage set, but modernism was spurned in favour of a novel combination of clothes and ephemera, quite literally purloined from granny's attic.

Like many other boutiques, its glory days were short – dogged by overheads and erratic stock levels, it rapidly became part of the London tourist trail, visitors stopping, if not to buy, simply to stand in amazement. The business lasted until 1969 when it was sold to Freddie Hornick who added a glam rock edge to the clothes, with New York and Los Angeles branches opening in the early 1970s.

OPPOSITE PAGE
Nigel Waymouth (right) and Michael Chaplin (son of Charlie) outside the first of many Granny Takes a Trip shop fronts, 1966.
TIME/Getty Images

OPPOSITE PAGE
The interior of Granny Takes a Trip
revolutionised boutique retailing, as
featured in *London Magazine*, October
1966.

NEXT SPREAD
One of the most memorable decorative
schemes of the sixties: Jean Harlow
graces the King's Road, 1967.
Rex Features

'Plum coloured walls, second-hand dresses, a black silk umbrella with tassels, coloured uniforms with their epaulettes and brass buttons, plants, stained 'glass' paper and bead curtains all make the texture of a picture that was intended, a picture seen through, so to speak, the fumes of Marijuana.'

Stephen Gardiner, *London Magazine*, October 1966

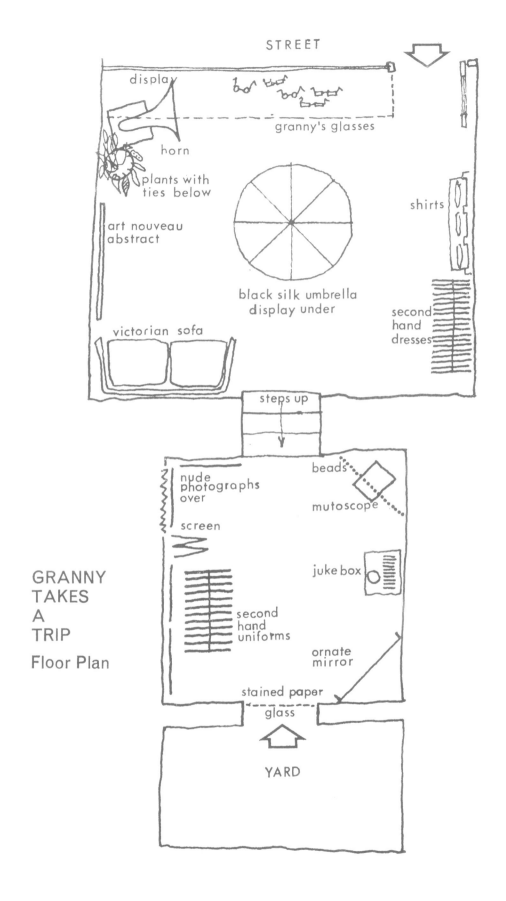

STREET

display

horn

plants with ties below

art nouveau abstract

granny's glasses

black silk umbrella display under

victorian sofa

shirts

second hand dresses

steps up

GRANNY TAKES A TRIP

Floor Plan

nude photographs over

screen

second hand uniforms

beads

mutoscope

juke box

ornate mirror

stained paper

glass

YARD

I Was Lord Kitchener's Valet

293 Portobello Road, W10

Like the huge portrait of Jean Harlow on the front of Granny Takes A Trip, the image of Lord Kitchener staring from the sign advertising I Was Lord Kitchener's Valet is one of the most powerful and evocative of the 1960s.

Run by John Paul and Robert Orbach, its success was not based on design and manufacture but on the ground-breaking recycling of elements of military and Victorian clothing into mainstream fashion.

It started as a market stall and evolved into a shop at 293 Portobello Road by 1966, the interior a dark and dense space combining 19th century military jackets, fur coats and Victorian junk into one huge nostalgic mix. Robert Orbach recalled in an interview for the *V&A* in 2006: 'I'm sitting there one morning and in walked John Lennon, Mick Jagger and Cynthia Lennon. And I didn't know whether I was hallucinating... but it was real. So Mick Jagger bought this tunic and wore it on *Ready Steady Go* when the Stones closed the show by performing *Paint it Black*. The next morning there was a line of about 100 people wanting to buy this tunic... and we sold everything in the shop by lunchtime.'

For many members of the general public the wearing of military uniform, particularly of identifiable rank, as a fashion accessory was a step too far. In September 1966 *The Times* reported from the Guildhall that a 'Muswell Hill youth' had been conditionally discharged after being stopped wearing a Scots Guards tunic. 'I think it looked fashionable and smart', the unnamed defendant commented. Davy Reeder, the manager of the Portobello shop told *The Times*: 'Our uniforms are all bought and sold legally and they are all obsolete so why shouldn't they be worn?'

OPPOSITE PAGE
Not everybody agreed with military uniform as a fashion accessory: a passer-by challenges a fashionably dressed couple on Carnaby Street, 1967.
Mirrorpix

OPPOSITE PAGE
I was Lord Kitchener's Valet began as a market stall selling uniforms, moving to 293 Portobello Road in 1966 then expanding into the West End.
David Graves/Rex Features

NEXT SPREAD
To illustrate Tom Salter's 1970 book on Carnaby Street, Malcolm English acknowledged the inspired adaptation of Lord Kitchener's recruitment poster to advertise the boutique.
Malcolm English

Success in Portobello Road meant ideas of expansion with branches in the West End, initially off Carnaby Street in Fouberts Place followed by a similar concession on Piccadilly Circus, ironically by then the cheaper of the two locations.

It was almost unimportant what the shops sold, such was their reputation for anti-establishment stunts. The Carnaby Street branch fell into trouble with the Lord Chamberlain for selling five shilling replicas of the Royal Coat of Arms, leftovers from the 1952 coronation celebrations. The shop had 3,000 inch-high emblems, 3,000 flags and 2,200 yards of bunting, but before the situation was resolved the stock had sold out.

John Paul went on to open I Was Lord Kitchener's Thing on the King's Road, inviting Chief Hunkeshnee (an honorary member of Sitting Bull's family) to attend the opening with a troupe of Red Indian dancers. Wearing traditional costumes and warpaint they marked the opening with the smoking of a ceremonial pipe and a performance of the Kolah dance, succeeding in fascinating and alarming the local residents in equal measure.

'A girl assistant was wearing a full dress jacket of the old Hertfordshire Regiment over skin-coloured tights, another customer was strutting around in black and gold "diplomatic gear".'

As it Happens reporter visits I Was Lord Kitchener's Valet in 1966

Apple Boutique

94 Baker Street, W1

In its all too brief existence the Apple Boutique managed to challenge the most elementary rules of retailing and experimented with ideas of communal design, even the very idea of ownership, but it will always be remembered as the Beatles' boutique.

Opened in December 1967, it employed a collective: 'The Fool', consisting of Dutch designers Simon Posthuma and Marijke Koeger, together with Simon Hayes and Barry Finch, with premises for the boutique secured at the junction of Baker Street and Paddington Street. The location, close to, but by no means in, the heart of shopping in the West End was an early indicator that Apple Boutique was different; when a huge and distinctive mural was painted on the outside of the building, a riot of rich psychedelic colour depicting a female fantasy figure, early indicators were confirmed.

The store had an eclectic staff drawn from varied associations with the band. John Lennon's friend Peter Shotton was manager and with Jenny Boyd, the sister of Mrs George Harrison, they sold fantasy clothes, loosely based on a stylised medieval aesthetic, but infused with the idealism behind the venture, together with the usual cocktail of nostalgia, drugs, music and psychedelia prevalent at the time.

Just as the collective had neglected to seek planning permission for the mural on the front of the building (being forced to paint it out in 1968 by Westminster Council) so too were the basics of running a business overlooked. Shoplifting was rife, partly because of the rules of the collective being somewhat ambiguous on the subject, partly because nobody could really stop it, such was the popularity of the band.

By July it was all over, and Apple announced that they would give away the stock. Huge crowds gathered in a stampede of interest which would have been an advertising agency's dream had the business intended to continue. On the first day, half of the stock (roughly 250 garments worth £3 each) was given away to teenagers, using the one item per person rule, with the remainder cleared the following day.

In the official press release in July 1968 Paul McCartney summarised the situation: 'We decided to close down our Baker Street shop yesterday and instead of putting up a sign saying "Business Will Be Resumed as Soon as Possible" and then auction off the goods, we decided to give them away. The shops were doing fine and making a nice profit on turnover. So far the biggest loss is in giving things away. But we did that deliberately. We came into the shops by the tradesman's entrance but we're leaving by the front door.'

OPPOSITE PAGE
Created in 1967, Apple Boutique's mural inspired strong feeling both for and against, eventually being painted over on the instructions of Westminster Council.
Bill Zygmant/Rex Features

OPPOSITE PAGE
Simon Posthuma and Marijke Koeger
modelling their own medieval-inspired
designs for Apple Boutique, 1967.
Topfoto

'A beautiful place where beautiful people can buy beautiful things.'

Paul McCartney, Apple Boutique, 1967

Dandie Fashions

161 King's Road, sw3

OPPOSITE PAGE
John and Andrea Crittle epitomised the glamorous and well connected clients of Dandie Fashions, which opened on the King's Road in 1966. *Daily Mail/Rex Features*

Dandie Fashions had everything expected of a menswear boutique catering for the like of the Beatles and Jimi Hendrix. The clothes were specifically designed with the modern dandy in mind – brocade, velvet, tapestry – a meeting of stage costume and bespoke tailoring that pre-empted the blurring of divisions between form, function and gender of the glam-rock era to come.

Neil Winterbotham, Alan Holston, John Crittle and the Hon. Tara Browne made up the quartet that opened Dandie Fashions in October 1966. Crittle had worked at Michael Rainey's Hung on You and the Hon. Tara Browne was half of the tailoring firm Foster & Tara which was already operating and supplying clothes to several well known boutiques in the area.

The boutique's location, closer to the mainstream run of shops on the King's Road around Top Gear and Countdown, chimed with Dandie Fashions intention to exploit its celebrity credentials and create a stopping-off point for fashion-conscious men, somewhere stylistically between the mainstream boutiques like John Michael and the more elitist and eclectic establishments around World's End.

Despite Browne's untimely death in a car accident in 1967, Dandie Fashions soon had a distinguished clientele and it had carved out a substantial niche market by the time Apple became interested in a collaborative venture in bespoke tailoring. As part of the agreement, Neil Aspinall and other members of the Beatles management team were appointed directors of Dandie Fashions, with John Crittle appointed to run the new venture, Apple Tailoring, in 1968.

The old and new guard on the
King's Road: Dandie Fashion's Art
Deco-inspired shop front by Binder,
Edwards and Vaughan, 1967.
Popperfoto/Getty Images

MORE SHOPS

Chelsea Antique Market
245a King's Road, sw3

An influential source for the boutiques in the area, selling everything and anything provided it was Victorian, including plumes, combs, birds in gilded cages, paintings, and junk from the £2 mark and upwards.

Earlybird
20 Park Walk, sw3

A Chelsea boutique selling clothes influenced by the establishments of World's End, featured in *London Magazine* in October 1966 as having a richly decorated interior on a par with Granny Takes a Trip.

GUY
170 King's Road, sw3

On the site of the first John Michael boutique and owned by the chain, a reasonably priced menswear boutique, noted in *Rave* magazine in 1966 as selling 'Battledress tops for boys in bright checks, casual wear and separates that match', all priced between 4 and 16 guineas.

Four:
Fashion Stars
Quorum/The Fulham Road Clothes Shop/
Annacat/Thea Porter

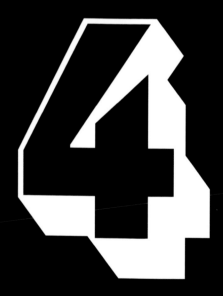

As London's boutique scene matured from the mid-1960s onwards, differences between the various approaches to selling began to become more apparent.

The pioneers meant business; Mary Quant, John Stephen and Foale and Tuffin existed to sell on their own terms both in London and across the globe, diversifying into international concessions. The majority of the World's End and Carnaby Street boutiques were about show; essentially experiments in retailing with no firm footing in manufacture or distribution which meant that, with the exception of Granny Takes a Trip, they remained peculiar to London. The third way was a mixture of the two, combining talented designers, buyers and retailers with boutique operations based on excellence, either in fashion and textile design or in the vision of the boutique's merchandise.

In some cases these came close to creative collectives: Quorum had the combined talents of Ossie Clark, Celia Birtwell and Alice Pollock and retailed in the King's Road area for almost a decade. Zandra Rhodes worked with Sylvia Ayton, with both excelling in their fields. Annacat resulted from the meeting of minds of Maggie Keswick and Janet Lyle.

All were linked by a star quality which, whilst not always a guarantee of financial success, reflected on London's boutique scene to great effect.

Quorum

21 Ansdell Street, w8
52 Radnor Walk, sw3
113 King's Road, sw3

Inspired by Hollywood glamour of the 1940s, a swing ticket for Ossie Clark's incredibly successful range of designs in association with Radley. *From the collection of Liz Eggleston*

OPPOSITE PAGE
Jane Asher wears an Ossie Clark paper dress in Celia Birtwell print surrounded by typical boutique eclectica, pictured for *Nova* in 1966. *Brian Duffy/Nova*

No other designer of the 1960s and 1970s had quite the glamour associated with Ossie Clark and his incredibly productive tenure at Quorum, the boutique owned by Alice Pollock.

He was another graduate of the inspirational Royal College of Art, where, encouraged by the likes of Bernard Nevill, he became well-versed in the skill of designers such as Madeleine Vionnet, forever associated with the perfection of the bias cut. His talent lay in his ability to produce designs that immediately flattered and that were so sensuous they pushed acceptable dress codes into new territory.

Quorum began life in Ansdell Street, near High Street Kensington, in 1964 and after an op-art inspired degree show catapulted him into the pages of *Vogue*, Ossie Clark was recruited to design for the boutique in 1965, with his partner Celia Birtwell producing textile designs. Alice Pollock allowed her co-designers freedom to work independently, but also provided a protective umbrella under which they had the practical benefits of work rooms, studios and a retail outlet. His first designs for Quorum drew on a modernist aesthetic; shift dresses with bands of contrasting colour trim at the hem and arms, with printed paper dresses following, allowing the talents of both he and his textile designer partner to flourish.

Quorum opened at 52 Radnor Walk in 1966, just off the King's Road in a largely residential street. It was to become a drawing room to the new 'Chelsea set' which was very different in tone to that celebrated by the press earlier in the decade. At its centre were Quorum's celebrity clients, drawn from the arts, music, fashion and aristocracy as before, but this time there was a hedonistic, self-destructive character that was heightened by the transient nature of fame. Everyone from Mick Jagger to Patti Boyd, David Hockney to Patrick Proctor were fans of Ossie Clark clothes.

With a boutique on the ground floor and the English Boy modelling agency on the first, Ossie Clark worked in a studio on the top floor, whilst Celia Birtwell produced a series of intense, vivid textiles designs at their home in Notting Hill. Very often working completely independently, fabric and design would meet in the studio and create clothes of exquisite beauty. From sell-out snakeskin biker jackets and coats to the transparent printed chiffons of the 'Nude look', Quorum provided a staple for Ossie Clark to thrive.

As with many creative ventures, notoriety did not necessarily translate into profit and by the late 1960s the business was in need of refinancing. A change in direction came with the sale of

Moss crepe tiered dress by Ossie Clark, £20 from Quorum, Spring/Summer 1971.
Fashion Museum, Bath

OPPOSITE PAGE
A winning team: evening dress by Ossie Clark in diaphanous chiffon print by Celia Birtwell, £45 from Quorum, Spring / Summer 1971.
Fashion Museum, Bath

Quorum to wholesaler Al Radley who was able to inject both capital and business acumen. Alice Pollock remained as director and Ossie Clark designed for two labels, the more expensive 'Ossie Clark for Quorum' and the affordable 'Ossie Clark for Radley' which became an instant success.

Suddenly the seductive glamour of rock stars and their girlfriends was made available to girls who had previously only dreamed of owning an Ossie Clark dress, and it was available in a Celia Birtwell print or fluid moss crepe. Radley provided Quorum with a smart new boutique at 113 King's Road in early 1969, with studios just around the corner in Burnsall Street, catapulting it from the small and intimate to centre stage in an international business.

Perhaps the zenith of Quorum's fame came in 1971 with a show at the Royal Court Theatre where celebrity models showed a new collection at a catwalk show that began at 2.30am, to an audience that included Paul and Linda McCartney and David Hockney. The boundaries between designers, models and celebrities had all merged and Quorum graduated from a boutique to an artistic salon of the cream of London's creative talent, but its decline was repeated many times over by similar businesses in the early 1970s as tastes and economics changed.

By 1972 the King's Road shop had closed as Ossie Clark became involved in his own label, leaving his designs for Radley to be adapted and re-worked by an in-house studio. At the same time, other designers including Betty Jackson and Sheridan Barnett were recruited, but the old magic was never recaptured, and Quorum was eventually completely absorbed into the Radley wholesale ready-to-wear empire.

'Ossie Clark is, I believe, in the world class for talent; in fact I think that we should build a completely modern idea of British high fashion around him.'

Prudence Glynn explaining her choice of an Ossie Clark ensemble for the Dress of the Year Award 1969

Sensuous and sophisticated, the chiffon
and moss crepe prints of Celia Birtwell
used to sublime effect by Ossie Clark.
Lichfield/Camera Press

The Fulham Road Clothes Shop

160 Fulham Road, sw6

OPPOSITE PAGE
Vanessa Redgrave strikes a pose
in a satin suit by The Fulham Road
Clothes Shop, the fabric design by
Zandra Rhodes reads 'We love you
Vanessa and send you kisses'.
Annette Green/Fashion Museum, Bath

As with Foale and Tuffin, a meeting of minds occurred when Zandra Rhodes and Sylvia Ayton opened the Fulham Road Clothes shop in 1968, backed by Vanessa Redgrave and Annette Green.

They had met at the Medway College of Art and both attended the Royal College of Art where Rhodes studied textile design, Ayton fashion. After Rhodes had success selling textile designs to Foale and Tuffin they decided that a boutique whereby they combined their talents was a natural progression.

Like many businesses which started during the decade, a combination of celebrity backers and rapid success ought to have meant a successful long-term business, but whilst the partnership had enough money to open and decorate a boutique, the day-to-day overheads were to prove too much, with both designers working in the shop and studio to keep the boutique running.

Their most distinctive range of clothes was a series of geometric prints on chiffon. Heavily influenced by pop art, the Rhodes design of an open lipstick proved a hit with fashion commentators, but was not enough to sustain a retail business and the boutique had closed by 1969.

Both partners were left with heavy losses, but went on to great success; Zandra Rhodes with her own fashion boutique and international collections, Sylvia Ayton as design head for the influential Wallis Shops.

OPPOSITE PAGE
Ossie Clark's favourite model
Gala Mitchell wears a satin and
organdie evening dress by Sylvia
Ayton in Zandra Rhodes lipstick
print, June 1968.
Annette Green/Fashion Museum, Bath

OVERLEAF
The place to see and be seen, the
King's Road in 1968.
Topfoto

SHOPS THIS WAY

Carnaby Street in all its glory as painted
by Malcolm English for Tom Salter's
history of the area, published in 1970.
Malcolm English

CARNABY

STREET

 SHOPS THIS WAY

Annacat

23 Pelham Street, SW3
270 Brompton Road, SW7

Annacat was run by Maggie Keswick and Janet Lyle and specialised in the new romanticism finding its way into fashion in the latter years of the sixties. 'Their clothes are charming, unexpected and wildly romantic', commented Prudence Glynn, featuring their high-necked velvet evening dresses trimmed with lace in *The Times* fashion pages.

This was a new kind of women's boutique, allied more with the traditional exclusivity of a salon, but still tuned in to the historical dressing up box being raided by the establishments at World's End. Above all they operated in a 'plush style' as *The Times* called it, a world away from the boutiques of Carnaby Street.

Opened in 1965 in Pelham Street, they sold their own designs with a small selection from other ready-to-wear houses, craft suppliers like Ritva knitwear, together with hats and accessories, all united by a nostalgia for an imagined romantic past. High-necked blouses, wide brimmed hats, velvets, printed georgette dresses with ties at the waist, all combined to represent the Annacat look.

The boutique had moved to larger premises on the Brompton Road by 1967 and became one of only a small number of such retailers to be regularly features in *Vogue*, *Queen* and most importantly the fashion editorials of Prudence Glynn and Ernestine Carter in *The Times* and *The Sunday Times* respectively.

Like Quorum and the bespoke menswear salons opening in Mayfair, Annacat had enough backing to show its collections like a fashion house, effectively blending boutique retailing and ready-to-wear and leading to phenomenal success in the late 1960s, culminating in the opening of a branch in New York in 1968.

The business continued into the next decade under various ownerships, retailing Annacat designs, dresses by Liberty, accessories by Guy Taplin and hats by Diane Logan and Sally Horton.

Sweet and simple, Annacat's advertising campaign for 1968.
From the collection of Liz Eggleston

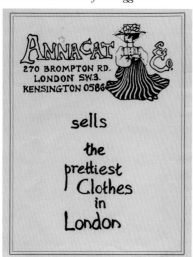

'Annacat sells the prettiest clothes in London.'

Annacat advertising slogan

Annacat promoted its designs in the same way as a couture house, but was essentially a boutique; Catherine Deneuve and David Bailey watch the show in December 1965.
Lichfield/Getty Images

Thea Porter
8 Greek Street, W1

Born in Jerusalem and raised in Syria, Thea Porter established Thea Porter Decorations on Greek Street in 1967, selling inlaid mother-of-pearl chests, paintings on glass, antiques found in street markets in Damascus, original kaftans and furnishings fabrics. She created her own souk amongst the coffee bars and wholesalers of Greek Street and soon began to design a range of exquisite clothes, incorporating elements of middle eastern dress, gypsy and art-historical references which complimented the late 1960s mood in fashion particularly well.

She travelled roughly four times a year, collecting stock and inspiration from the markets and antique dealers she visited, translating them into her clothes. Using fine brocades, tulles and lamé fabrics, embroidery and butterfly wing colours, she soon attracted a substantial following of celebrity clients including Elizabeth Taylor, Bianca Jagger, Barbra Streisand and Princess Margaret.

Her clothes were luxurious, coveted and particularly well suited to eveningwear, lying somewhere between the sleekness of Ossie Clark and the layered and complex clothes of Bill Gibb, the most repeated forms being based on the fluidity and drape of the traditional kaftan.

Further shops followed as Thea Porter Decorations became Thea Porter Couture, with a concession within Henri Bendel in New York added in 1969, the influential I Magin department store in San Francisco, together with Giorgio of Beverley Hills on Rodeo Drive and a stand-alone boutique in Paris in 1976.

OPPOSITE PAGE AND OVERLEAF
Thea Porter designs for Spring 1972 combining fluid, exotic prints with simple tailored and draped shapes, photographed by John Cowan for Ernestine Carter at *The Sunday Times*. *John Cowan/Fashion Museum, Bath*

'Of course it's agony trying to organise deliveries and I never quite know what to expect when parcels arrive.'

Thea Porter interviewed for *Monday Merry-Go-Round* in June 1967

MORE SHOPS

Antiquarius
131-141 Kings Road, SW3

A rambling barn of 150 stalls, it sold everything from Georgian snuff boxes to 1930s copies of *Vogue* along with one of the largest selections of Victorian, Edwardian and later clothing in a room with a stained glass ceiling. Businesses of particular note in the early 1970s included Melodie and Sally Mee Textiles, both dealing in vintage clothing and cited as being popular with designers like Ossie Clark.

Browns
27 South Molton Street, W1

The influential boutique opened in 1970 by Joan and Sidney Burstein to showcase the very best in design talent. It rapidly expanded to include adjacent properties in the street and encouraged the addition of South Molton Street as a shopping destination of note, one of the very few boutiques still operating in its original form.

Vanessa Frye
6 Sloane Street, SW1

Exotic and ultra-fashionable women's clothing from UK designers and further afield, selected by Vanessa Denza of Woollands 21 fame and opened in 1966. Stockist of Tipper-Ipper-Appa clothes, designed by Lesley Kermot (who had worked for Granny Takes a Trip) and Judy Scutt, made up from vintage textiles and trim.

Vidal Sassoon
44 Sloane Street, SW1

For a brief period London's favourite hairdresser incorporated clothes into his salon on Sloane Street. With stock selected by Lady Rendlesham it opened in October 1968, stocking capsule collections from, amongst others, V de V, Ossie Clark and Foale and Tuffin.

Five:
Made to Measure
Mr Fish/Blades/The House of Nutter

The image of the 1960s male dandy has long been associated with the boutiques of the King's Road and Carnaby Street at their most influential, but it was also cultivated in the exclusive salons of a handful of Mayfair designers and tailors, the most widely influential of which has to have been Mr Fish.

Michael Fish drew on the extremes of style seen at the likes of Hung on You, the Apple Boutique and Dandie Fashions and combined them with the expertise of traditional Savile Row tailoring, essentially creating a bespoke boutique look. In his case innovations went much further, taking design to extremes on a number of occasions, with other more traditional tailors intergrating selected innovations into their ranges.

Rupert Lycett-Green's Blades provided the crème de la crème of London society with the finest money could buy; this was couture for men at its most glamorous. Tommy Nutter took traditional tailoring and bumped it into the next decade with changes in pattern and cut, but with an essential respect for the design form.

Everybody, it seemed, wanted to take part in what the press collectively termed the 'Peacock Revolution'.

Michael Fish revolutionised menswear
design and retailing, opening Mr Fish in
1966; the interior was part gentlemen's
club, part boutique.
John Lyons/Rex Features

Mr Fish

17 Clifford Street, w1

Michael Fish stormed the barricades of the unsuspecting world of bespoke menswear and opened Mr Fish in Clifford Street, Mayfair in 1966. Always associated with the outrageous and controversial, his menswear designs took historically inspired tailoring to a new level whilst establishing a cult following amongst the rock and pop aristocracy of London.

His signature was the brightly coloured, beautifully tailored suit of the new London dandy, and with it came vivid printed ties, ruffle fronted silk shirts trimmed with lace and kaftans for men, all sold from his exotically furnished salon which combined the atmosphere of a Pall Mall club with an upmarket nightclub.

He had begun his career at Turnbull and Asser in 1962, but it was an invitation to a party by a customer that was to profoundly affect his career. Barry Sainsbury suggested there was a need for a boutique selling upmarket, fashionable clothes for men and said that if Michael Fish could provide the ideas, he would provide the backing.

What followed was a boutique of legend – even the opening party was filmed by an Italian television crew documenting what they perceived as the fall of the British aristocracy. His designs inspired strong feelings for and against, but like many successful fashion designers, the controversial designs attracted a publicity which enabled a core business to flourish.

By the time he was interviewed by Antony King Deacon in December 1969, the business already had an annual turnover of £250,000 and he had been in the headlines for his smock dress worn by Mick Jagger at the Stones Hyde Park concert the previous July. 'When people attack me for putting mini skirts on men, or if Mick Jagger is photographed wearing one of my outrageous numbers and I am critised for thinking up such stupidity, I tell them that I am happy, that I don't interfere with them. People get hung-up about fashion but it's really not important.'

This was a new kind of dressing, combining the craftsmanship of traditional London tailoring with ethnic references from the near and middle east, the hippies and the Regency dandy. Lord Snowdon, the Beatles and the Rolling Stones all embraced this technicolour revolution; even John Pertwee as *Doctor Who* wore a ruffle-fronted Mr Fish shirt.

Appealing to similar sections of fashionable London society, Annacat and Mr Fish joined forces for a fashion show at the Playboy Club in February 1968.
From the collection of Liz Eggleston

OPPOSITE PAGE
Hyde Park 1969: Mick Jagger recites
an excerpt from Shelley's elegy *Adonais*
in memory of band member Brian Jones,
the Mr Fish smock causing controversy
in the press the following day.
Robert Hunt/Rex Features

'I do my own thing, and I am happy doing it.'

Michael Fish interviewed by Antony King Deacon in 1969

OPPOSITE PAGE
James Fox dressed by Mr Fish
in dice motif dinner jacket for his
role in the film *Duffy* (1968).
Fashion Museum, Bath

NEXT SPREAD
By the late 1960s the likes of
Mr Fish and Blades had changed
the look of fashionable menswear
forever, expunging dark traditional
suiting in favour of exotic fabrics,
colour and pattern.
Malcolm English

Blades

8 Burlington Gardens, W1

OPPOSITE PAGE AND OVERLEAF
Suits by Blades for 1965: the firm swiftly
adapted to the menswear revolution
tailoring some of the most beautifully
made and fashionable clothes of the
late 1960s.

If Mr Fish accentuated the menswear revolution, Blades interpreted and adapted the new styles for a discerning clientele. Described in the 1970 edition of *London on $500 a Day*, the guide for American visitors, as 'somewhere between Savile Row and Bohemia, pop and gentleman combined, London's outstanding fashion store for the young man, 35/40 down, depending what shape you're in.'

Founded by Rupert Lycett-Green, Blades had been established for a number of years before moving from Dover Street to the former premises of A J Whites hatters in Burlington Gardens by 1967. Almost immediately the press took note of the newcomers. 'The most important aspect of making clothes is that people should wear them', Rupert Lycett-Green told the papers the same year, and true to his word he perfected a look that became associated with Blades. Jackets were long and lean, tailored to hug the figure, the shoulders natural. Pockets were emphasised to balance the lapels, trousers very slightly flared. The Blades formula could be repeated in almost any fabric, damask or velvet for evening, more traditional wools for daywear.

Interviewed by the *V&A* in 2006, interior designer David Mlinarc recalled his restoration of the largely 18th century building for Blades: 'We stripped out, as I nearly always do, everything that had been put in since the original building date, and we put practically nothing back in. We simply mended things and lit from a low level. They sold hats as well as suits and we got some heads like you put on mannequins, stuck newspaper on them and hung them up on the wall, about twenty of them, and that's what you saw when you came in. All the clothes were just on hangers on rails. It's not unconventional now but then things would usually be in display cases. The shop had a front door and a staircase and was quite like a house really, it was quite club-like.'

In March 1969 Blades held a fashion show in Burlington Gardens, widely reported by the press as definitive of the period in menswear. Guests included a selection of the cast of Hair, with Martha Hunt and also the critic Kenneth Tynan. The suits on show blended the usual wearable shapes from Blades with the finest Indian silks and had embroidery around the hems of the jackets.

Some menswear editors regarded the peacock fashions of Mayfair in the late 1960s as gaudy self-publicity, but Blades weathered the menswear storm by adhering to the principals of its founders, moving successfully into ready-to-wear in 1970 whilst still maintaining its select bespoke operation.

'There is nothing in all London as elegant and as wearable as the simple Blades suit.'

The Times March 1969

Dedicated followers of fashion,
the Rolling Stones take a stroll
in Green Park photographed by
Dezo Hoffmann in 1967.
Dezo Hoffmann/Rex Features

The House of Nutter

35a Savile Row, W1

Whereas many menswear designers in late 1960s wanted to introduce high fashion into bespoke tailoring, Tommy Nutter wanted to introduce bespoke tailoring into high fashion, for he was a fan of the suit.

His approach was to take what already existed in classic menswear design and to refine and exaggerate only certain aspects, not the entirety. Lapels on jackets became extra-wide, combinations of check and dogtooth motifs became more daring, and the scale of pattern repeats became larger, creating a distinctive Tommy Nutter look. 'If you see dog's tooth tweed trousers and a Prince of Wales tweed jacket beautifully blended in colour and pattern, they were most likely born at Tommy Nutter's,' commented one guide to London shopping in 1970.

Backed by Cilla Black and Peter Brown of Apple, the House of Nutter opened at 35a Savile Row in 1969, a combination of a bespoke tailors' workroom and a boutique, one of the first where the construction of suits could be seen from the street.

He worked with the traditionally trained tailor Edward Sexton, and together they took the bastion of British bespoke menswear by surprise, creating their refreshing and unusual suits. The Beatles wore House of Nutter on the cover of Abbey Road as did a certain Bianca Pérez Morena de Macías for her St Tropez wedding in 1971.

In the mid-1970s Tommy Nutter launched a new venture under his own-name label at 19 Savile Row, this time re-working the classic tailoring of the 1930s which had by then returned to vogue. His collections included plus-fours, Norfolk jackets, huge window-pane checks and exaggerated 'Gatsby' caps.

'The classic suit is here to stay – with a little more design applied to it.'

Tommy Nutter interviewed by Andrew Phillips, May 1969

Tommy Nutter pictured at his Savile Row shop in 1969: he brought fashion to bespoke tailoring and was backed by Cilla Black and Peter Brown of Apple. *Jones/Getty Images*

MORE SHOPS

Apple Tailoring (Civil and Theatrical)
161 Kings Road, SW3

Apple Tailoring joined the Apple boutique as one of the Beatles' brief experiments in retailing in 1968. Opening in the same premises as Dandie Fashions and run by John Crittle, the intention was to sell bespoke tailoring along with a hairdressing salon run by the group's stylist Leslie Cavendish in the basement. In reality the venture fell victim to poor sales and the changing priorities of the group, closing within the year.

Apple Tailoring opened in the same premises as Dandie Fashions but joined the Apple Boutique as a short lived experiment in retailing.
Andrew Maclear/Getty Images

The Chelsea Cobbler
The Studio, 18 Emperor's Gate, SW3
163 Draycott Avenue, SW3
33 Sackville Street, W1

Owned by Richard Smith and Mandy Wilkins and opened in 1967, The Chelsea Cobbler made the finest bespoke shoes for men and women, chosen from their extensive catalogue. They were designed to be worn with the outfits of Thea Porter, Mr Fish or Tommy Nutter and came in brightly coloured and exotic materials including suede, lizard and snakeskin.

Tom Gilbey
36 Sackville Street, W1

Tom Gilbey opened just off Piccadilly in 1968 and joined the ranks of Britain's finest menswear designers with rapid success and regular appearances in the line-up of catwalk shows. A particular speciality were the sleekly-cut safari and military looks popular in the early 1970s.

Six:
Carnaby Street Welcomes the World
The John Stephen Empire/Lord John/
Lady Jane/Irvine Sellars/Gear

As *Time* magazine declared London the centre of the world in 1966, Carnaby Street crammed the experience of being young and fashionable into just a few hundred yards, an extra strong dose of what the press perceived to be 'Swinging London', the tightly-packed shopping streets to either side heightening the effect. Some style commentators at the time, however, sensed that a tide was turning and that the nature of Carnaby Street was changing, not necessarily for the better.

The second half of the decade saw the rise of retailing as theatre and ultimately Carnaby Street led the way in the deliberate courting of controversy in order to gain the attention of the press. Stunts included sales girls in their underwear, half-naked models in the window, even a girl hoisted aloft in a birdcage in a triumph of style over design substance.

Although perceived by the press as the heart of the creative capital, many of the boutiques were reinventions of shops which had thrived in other locations. I was Lord Kitchener's Valet added a branch in Carnaby Street and later in Piccadilly Circus and the King's Road enabling it to sell to customers who would never have ventured to Portobello. Boutiques were diffused and multiplied, essentially following the model of John Stephen who argued that even though he might be competing against himself to some extent, a sale would eventually occur in one of his boutiques as a result.

A new type of businessman characterised the boutique owners of W1, among them Harry Fox with his Lady Jane chain and Warren and David Gold with Lord John. They realised that what their customers were looking for was a chance to buy into the increasingly publicised and ironically fragmented 'youth market'. The boutiques that had broken new ground were now well established or had even moved on, but Carnaby Street gave a taste of them to the masses.

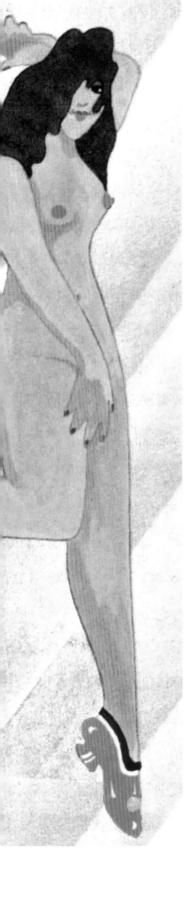

Alongside the clothes and shoe shops, new ventures such as Kleptomania and Gear provided the eclectic mix of Victoriana, Union Jack merchandise and souvenirs. The explosion in the taste for Victoriana had started with the decoration of the World's End boutiques and, combined with the fact that it was still readily available in London's street markets, provided an ironic comment by the young and stylish on the 'establishment' and the age of Empire. It also marked an increasing interest in the design of the 19th century, particularly in Art Nouveau and the work of artists such as Aubrey Beardsley, whose overt eroticism and humour seemed fresh and new after the starkness of modernism.

The George Melly scripted film *Smashing Time* (1967) starring Lynn Redgrave and Rita Tushingham provided biting satire of fashionable London as he saw it. His heroines arrive in the capital from the north with dreams of fame and fortune but enter a bizarre, and above all temporary, world of celebrity and high fashion, such a vivid and brilliant cocktail of opportunity, wealth and vulgarity that their eventual return to reality is welcomed by both. Rita Tushingham's character even finds a job in the fictional Too Much boutique of Chelsea, whose owner lives in fear of selling anything and interrupting her social life. With a delicious sense of irony, George Melly chose a boutique on Carnaby Street for the film's launch party.

Carnaby Street provided fun and fashion in equal measure, as illustrated by Malcolm English in the late 1960s.
Malcolm English

The John Stephen Empire

Carnaby Street, W1

9 John Stephen Tailoring
38 Male W1
41 HIS Clothes, later HIS 'N' HERS
46 Trecamp
46a Domino Male
47a Mod Male, later Adam W1
49/51 John Stephen Manshop
52-55 John Stephen Store

HIS Clothes

189 Regent Street, W1
40 Old Compton Street, W1
201 King's Road, SW3
63 Queensway, W2
171 Earls Court Road, SW3

John Stephen

33 Old Bailey, EC4
97 King's Road, SW3

OPPOSITE PAGE
John Stephen and model at his Trecamp
boutique in 1967, the changing rooms
were decorated by Myles Anthony with
life-size photographs of bodybuilders.
Dezo Hoffmann/Rex Features

Ever since his first boutique on Carnaby Street in the late 1950s it was apparent that John Stephen's approach to business was unique. The level of expansion associated with his main brands was unprecedented: by the end of the 1960s he had multiple stores on and around Carnaby Street, Regent Street and the King's Road, several boutiques outside London, as well as some in the USA and Europe.

From the start he argued that competing against himself was his intention. By 1966, in an effort to increase sales space, and as a telling indicator of just how many properties on the street he owned, he was knocking adjacent premises together so that shoppers could pass between boutiques without leaving the building.

In 1967 he proved he knew what girls wanted too and introduced womenswear into his Trecamp Boutique, the changing rooms of which were decorated with life-size photographs of bodybuilders by designer Myles Anthony. The John Stephen Store at 52-55 Carnaby Street later ran to three floors, with the first reserved for girls, and a café in the basement.

Branches of HIS clothes opened in Earls Court, Bayswater, even in Brighton, mirroring the other London boutique export to the city, Biba. John Stephen shops opened in the USA on the delayed shockwaves of the 'Youthquake' explosion, with re-branded 'Carnaby' boutiques in Italy, Sweden, Norway, West Germany, and the island of Ischia.

In many ways the simplicity of his marketing technique was a precursor to what is generally accepted as the norm today. From small beginnings he expanded, and expanded further, diversifying as the core businesses began to support themselves. From there he exported a little piece of Carnaby Street to the world, eventually adding his own large-scale manufacturing facilities in Glasgow.

Perhaps his most significant legacy to retailing is the way in which he understood that celebrity approval was the key to beginning and shaping trends which he could meet. The creation of the John Stephen Fashion award for the best dressed man in 1964 meant that a huge crowd and pages of publicity for his boutiques, were guaranteed every year.

The brand continued until the mid-1970s, eventually being sold to competitors at the same time that Carnaby Street was generally accepted to have seen better days. John Stephen himself came full circle, opening the Francisco-M boutique chain, again selling continental menswear to appreciative Londoners, eventually securing the exclusive British franchise for Lanvin menswear.

OPPOSITE PAGE
One of an increasing number of John
Stephen-owned boutiques on Carnaby
Street, Male West One pictured in 1966.
Petra Niemeier/Getty Images

'He made Carnaby Street.
He was Carnaby Street.
He invented a look for young
men which was wildly
exuberant, dashing and fun.'

Mary Quant interviewed by *The Independent*, September 2005

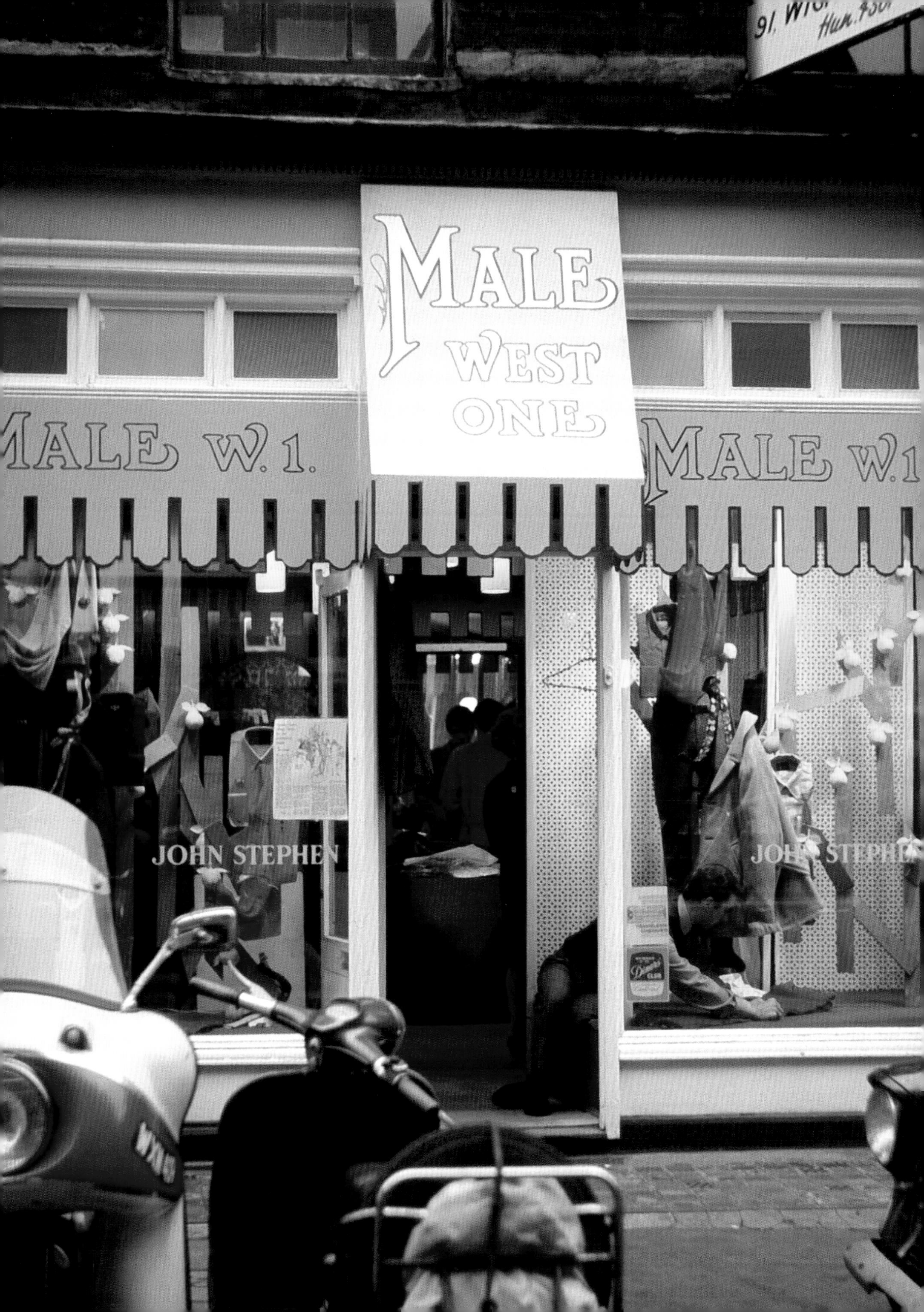
MALE
WEST
ONE
MALE W. 1.
MALE W. 1
JOHN STEPHEN

Dominating the Carnaby Street scene: Lord John's mural by Binder, Edwards and Vaughan made it one of the most photographed buildings on the street. *Clive McLean/Rex Features*

Lord John

43 Carnaby Street, W1
27-28 Great Marlborough Street, W1

Warren and David Gold mirrored John Stephen in their incredible rise from humble beginnings to success on Carnaby Street and beyond. They began retailing on Petticoat Lane, which like Portobello Road combined a sea of Victorian bric-a-brac with clothing and a general street market. There they had such success selling suede jackets and coats that they were able to open two shops around Carnaby Street starting in 1964, but continued to trade on Petticoat Lane even after acquiring a Rolls Royce. 'The Rolls is useful when it's getting dark David Gold explained, 'I focus the headlights onto the stall so the customers can see the colours properly.'

Purportedly called Lord John after Warren Gold's nickname at school, the boutiques specialised in the 'mod' look that swept through menswear in the mid-1960s. Lord John was particularly adept at ensuring that they always had versions of the latest trends for sale, and at securing the patronage of male pop stars, thereby maximising publicity in the music and fashion press.

Their success and eventual expansion of the brand mirrors that of many other retailers as opposed to designers at the time, whose ability to react to the ever-changing men's fashion scene rapidly, and to undercut on price, put them at a distinct advantage. The Gold brothers' skill for spotting the latest trends also ran to decoration: in 1967 they commissioned David Vaughan, Douglas Binder and Dudley Edwards to decorate the exterior of the Lord John branch on the corner of Ganton Street and Carnaby Street with a huge psychedelic mural, making it easily one of the most photographed buildings of the street.

Lady Jane
Lady Jane's Birdcage
Lady Jane Again

28, 29 & 36 Carnaby Street

The series of Lady Jane boutiques were the brainchild of Harry Fox and Henry Moss and marked the start of the arrival of womenswear retailers in the Carnaby Street area in increasing numbers, with the original Lady Jane opened in 1966. The Lady Jane team were masters of showmanship and ever more daring stunts were unveiled to increase publicity.

For the Lady Jane launch catsuit clad models in the windows led to Henry Moss being fined £2 plus 20 guineas costs for causing an obstruction, whilst at the opening of Lady Jane's Birdcage a bikini-clad girl was suspended twenty feet above the street in the appropriate cage. Huge crowds soon gathered and the police subsequently repeated the charge of causing an obstruction. At the hearing the judge, Mr St John Harmsworth, was quoted as saying 'You set up a good promotion, but try to be less exuberant. In the circumstances, I cannot find it in my heart to fine you.'

Lady Jane Again opened in 1969, selling the by now familiar mix of Carnaby Street merchandise – a combination of reasonably priced copies of high fashion combined with designs plucked from a hedonistic mixing of cultures and styles, as modernism was left far behind.

As early as 1967 Henry Moss was writing to *The Times* in protest at the proposed pedestrianisation of the street citing that 'London thrives on its streets being choked with traffic' and that 'people only come to Carnaby Street in such numbers because they can be taken there in a taxi'. He also explained that deliveries to and from the Lady Jane boutiques would be affected. Various experiments with traffic control were conducted from the late 1960s, but Carnaby Street was not officially pedestrianised until 1973, with the addition of a mosaic of brightly coloured rubberised paving stones, in some way an attempt to reflect the vibrant nature of its immediate history. The move was generally agreed even at the time to be a mistake, permanently changing the atmosphere of the area.

Only Lady Jane would think of locking a girl in a birdcage to publicise a boutique, illustrated in the late 1960s by artist Malcolm English.
Malcolm English

Irvine Sellars
Mates

27 & 25 Carnaby Street, W1

OPPOSITE PAGE
Irvine Sellar's boutique Mates opened in Carnaby Street in the mid 1960s, selling both men's and women's clothes in the same shop for the first time.
ITV/Rex Features

For a brief period it seemed that Carnaby Street had the ability to make fortunes almost overnight. It was simply a question of finding and exploiting a demand, the crowds thronging up and down outside hoping to bump into Mick Jagger, The Who or Mary Quant would do the rest.

Irvine Sellars came closest to matching John Stephen in the scope and size of his boutique empire with 24 boutiques by the age of 32 in 1969. He started in the mid-1950s with a small stall on Hitchin market, eventually expanding into Petticoat Lane selling large quantities of clothing by employing three managers. 'It's the hardest living in the world working the markets, but it's the best training,' he told fashion journalist Erica Crone in 1969.

Several retail outlets followed, including one in St Albans, another in Wood Green, then Wardour Street, before he arrived in Carnaby Street in the early 1960s with a boutique called Tom Cat. He noticed that girls were increasingly accompanying their boyfriends on shopping trips, sometimes buying men's clothes themselves. So he combined fashions for both men and women in the highly successful Mates chain, with his other boutiques including Carnaby Girl and his own-name store.

Mates was expanded into all the main shopping areas of London by the late 1960s, with Sellars accurately predicting changes in retailing, including the introduction of new synthetic fabrics and more open-plan shopping. Like John Stephen and his factory in Glasgow, Sellar's success was compounded by the fact that he manufactured around 70% of the clothes sold in his stores using his own group of companies.

Gear

35 Carnaby Street, W1

OPPOSITE PAGE
Gear was an Aladdin's cave of Victorian furniture and eclectic junk owned by Tom Salter, who opened on Carnaby Street thanks to the encouragement of John Stephen.
Clive McLean/Rex Features

Tom Salter's arrival on Carnaby Street was largely due to the encouragement of his friend John Stephen, who dissuaded him from opening his home furnishings store in Henley and convinced him that Carnaby Street was the place to be. He created an Aladdin's cave of Victorian furniture, stripped pine and junk, first opening in the early 1960s, and gradually expanding to larger premises.

Interviewed by Victoria Potter in 2008, he recalled 'We were so busy, I didn't have enough stuff to fill the shop. I guess in those days, I thought business was like that and everybody was that busy. I was selling large pieces like pine chests and Welsh dressers, and I remember I had this big Welsh dresser and the main reason for it was it blocked half the shop, so nobody knew there was empty space behind it! Donovan was one of our first celebrity customers – I think I sold him a chair. Eventually, we sold to everybody – The Beatles, The Stones, Marianne Faithfull, Liberace and so forth.'

Over a relatively short period of time he managed to achieve enormous success and proved that visitors to Carnaby Street were keen to take a little piece of it away with them as a souvenir. 'As Carnaby Street started to pick up, it became clear that I needed to sell more small things, because not everyone was going to walk off with these pieces of Victoriana, so we started selling smaller pieces and eventually became a gift and souvenir shop.' To that was added Kids in Gear in the basement with clothes designed by Carol Payne, children descending to the store via a helter-skelter, parents by the stairs.

Like many boutiques that sold flags and coats of arms to tourists, Gear ran into trouble with the authorities (in this case the American embassy) when they hung the Stars and Stripes over their doorway, eventually having to replace it with a Union Jack.

Diversification and expansion, even on the same street, were the order of the day in the latter half of the 1960s and Salter was involved with a number of other brightly painted boutiques on the street, including Pop and Kleptomania, and The Great Gear Trading Company on the King's Road. In 1970 he published what has proved to be one of very few comprehensive recollections of Carnaby Street, with psychedelic illustrations by the artist Malcolm English.

Adam
29 Kingley Street, WI

A small menswear boutique renowned for trousers in every conceivable style, one of the first boutiques in the area, with prices from 3 to 6 guineas a pair in the late 1960s.

Aristos
45 Carnaby Street, WI

Opened by Aristos Constantinou in 1966 designing and retailing womenswear, the business expanded significantly into the wholesale ready-to-wear market in the early 1970s with well-produced copies of couture fashion, eventually securing stockists worldwide.

Kleptomania
22 Carnaby Street, WI

Originally opened in direct competition with Gear it was run by Charlie Simpson and Tommy Roberts who paid £18,000 for a lease. Selling a heady mix of fashion, junk, kaftans and hippy bells it eventually joined forces with Gear as Tommy Roberts went on to open the Mr Freedom boutique on the King's Road.

Pussy Galore
5,6 & 7 Carnaby Street, WI

Women's boutique named after the James Bond heroine, opened in 1969 by Henry Moss following the end of his business partnership with Harry Fox. By the early 1970s came Sweet Fanny Adams with both boutiques associated with the usual risqué publicity stunts at regular intervals.

Ravel
22 & 44 Carnaby Street, WI

Shoes for men and women, owned by Raoul Chaussures of Oxford Street, ultimately opening three branches on Carnaby Street and stores throughout the UK.

MORE SHOPS

Simon Shop
2 New Burlington Street, W1

One of the first of a generation of wig boutiques opening in the mid 1960s, with prices in 1966 ranging from £20 to £150.

Sportique
63 Old Compton Street, W1

Slightly to the east of Carnaby Street, Sportique was recommended in several mid-1960s shopping guides for their belts in all colours of the rainbow and for a wide range suede jackets, the most expensive at 26 guineas.

Take 6
24 Carnaby Street and branches

A highly-successful middle-market menswear chain owned by Sidney Brent, with 14 branches throughout London selling a full range of modern styles following the John Stephen model.

Topper Shoes
45 Carnaby Street, W1

To go with the clothes, men's and women's shoes designed by Steve Topper, prices ranged from just over £2 to around £7.

Wild West Won
16a D'Arblay Street, W1

As the name suggested a specialist in the American look, selling 'sporty' checked shirts in Indian cotton at 49s 11d, with the most expensive items at around 9 guineas.

Seven:
The Domino Effect

London's boutiques had, until the late 1960s, normally fallen into one of two categories. The designer/retailers marketed and sold their own clothes in the modern equivalent of a ready-to-wear salon, brought up to date by more affordable prices, the addition of a shop front and a jukebox. The retail boutiques acted as connoisseurs, cherry-picking from fashion houses, junk markets and craft producers to stock their own personal vision of where fashion was at any one given time. The shop-in-a-shop or boutique concession within department stores brought a third way, and with it an explosion in manufacturing and sponsorship deals, all of which aimed to capture a little of the boutique magic of the King's Road, Carnaby Street and all stations in between.

The earliest and perhaps the most influential in London had been Vanessa Denza's 21 shop opened in 1961 at Woollands in Knightsbridge, which had transformed the fortunes of the entire department store by allowing it to shed its traditional image. Peter Robinson had Top Shop by 1964 which germinated into a high street chain in the early 1970s. Selfridges opened Miss Selfridge in 1966 and counted Zandra Rhodes and Sylvia Ayton as designers of a line of paper dresses; by 1967 concessions had blossomed in Lewis's department stores country-wide with high street branches by 1969. The list of other major retailers entering the game by the late 1960s is substantial: Austin Reed's attempt was Cue; Simpson's, Trend; there was Young Jaeger; and Harrods' Way In. Importantly, and unlike previous attempts to sell clothes to younger clients, the stores deliberately attempted to replicate the atmosphere, as they perceived it, of the independent boutiques with sales areas often in darker basements or brightly decorated with a diffused psychedelic palette. Ironically it worked, and brought at least a spirit of boutique retailing to a far greater audience than would have ever made the journey to central London to see the originals.

Following hot on the heels of the proliferation of boutique retailing came the sponsorship deals with models and pop stars of the period to endorse clothing ranges. Between 1966 and 1968 Twiggy, Cathy McGowan and Sandie Shaw all signed on the dotted line to put their name to fashion brands, with varying degrees of involvement. Twiggy 'oversaw' a design team and the clothes were displayed in a variety of fashionable stockists on Twiggy portrait hangers.

Cathy McGowan's Boutique-labelled designs were specifically retailed by the GUS mail order empire and were designed to reflect her *Ready Steady Go* style. With the slogan 'What every girl wants to be', sales rose from 50,000 per season on launching

OPPOSITE PAGE
By the late 1960s even mainstream department stores such as D H Evans embraced the psychedelic imagery of the boutiques.
Fashion Museum, Bath

A fashion heroine to a generation, Cathy McGowan launched her own range of mail order fashion in 1966, selling the simple mod shapes she was famous for wearing on *Ready Steady Go*. *From the collection of Liz Eggleston*

to over 200,000 by 1968, the same year that Sandie Shaw promoted a capsule collection of her label for sale via a variety of stockists.

At the same time came what are today often referred to as 'Boutique' labels, designers manufacturing and selling in the same circles as the well-known retailers of the time, but who never ran their own boutiques. A notable example was Gerald McCann who was extremely successful from the early 1960s; a later one, Rae Spencer-Cullen with her Miss Mouse brand, exploited the same sense of risqué fun as Mr Freedom.

Following on from all this diffusion were the wholesale ready-to-wear manufacturers, literally hundreds of different firms who reproduced whatever they knew they could sell to regional and suburban department stores, boutiques and dress shops. Among the most successful of the period were Quad, Mr Darren and Dollyrockers, ironically in many cases producing clothes that, because they were factory-made, had a better standard of finish than the hastily assembled high fashion designs they were copying.

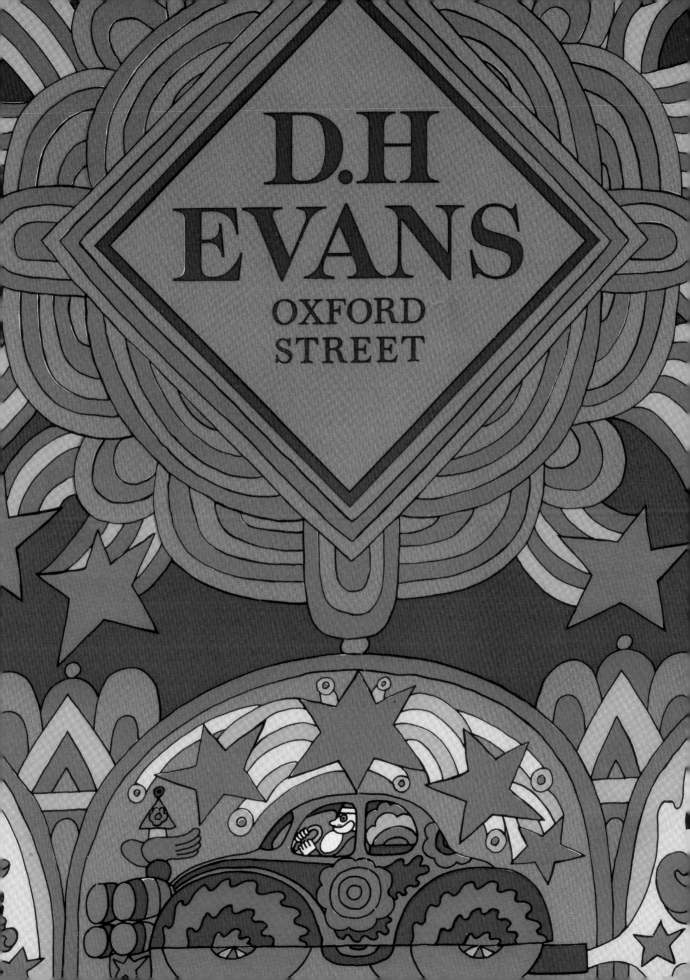

Eight:
Adventures in Glamour
Mr Freedom/Cobblers to the World/
Big Biba/Zapata

OVERLEAF
Members of Chelsea FC join the models
and take a turn in Mr Freedom's 1940s
casino-themed collection for Spring/
Summer 1973; from left to right: Ian
Hutchinson, Cindy Cartmel, Alan
Hudson, Suze, Steve Kember, Myna
Bird and Bill Garner.
Stringer/Getty Images

If the mid-1960s proved that the formula of combining a young designer with a rundown shop usually worked and produced a successful boutique, the latter years of the decade tested the assumption that big was beautiful and, usually, glamorous.

The majority of the boutiques in central London had to date been relatively modest in size, ranging from the cupboard sized Top Gear to slightly larger; the most expansive in the late 1960s was probably Biba or the larger John Stephen stores.

Kensington High Street hosted the new stars, mainly because, unlike the King's Road and Carnaby Street, larger premises were available to rent, a situation made possible by the first casualties amongst department stores as shopping tastes began to change.

The new names like Mr Freedom and Big Biba certainly needed the space, as London witnessed shopping as theatre, a glittering circus where the clothes and the shopping environment became props in a larger production, taken to extremes in both cases. Whether they were still boutiques in the true sense of the word is debateable, but both had started small and gone on to bigger and better things, taking the same customers with them and adding others.

Meanwhile, and on a smaller scale, retailers and designers centred mainly around the King's Road made accessories to go with the finery or opened increasingly polished and sophisticated venues to sell the clothes as boutique retailing in London entered a dramatic new phase.

Mr Freedom

430 King's Road, sw3
20 Kensington Church Street, w8

By the late 1960s it seemed that everything that could be done had been done when it came to boutiques. Tommy Roberts and Trevor Myles proved this wrong, however, and took fashion into new territory, challenging the existing shops on the King's Road with an exercise in fantasy and showmanship as never seen before.

Opened in 1968 on the site of Hung on You and backed by John Paul and Ian Fiske of I Was Lord Kitchener's Valet, they combined pop art and Americana in a riot of a boutique, selling giant platforms, t-shirt dresses appliquéd with stars, a bizarre combination of Wild West cowgirl and rock star glamour that was as novel as the short, sharp shapes of the mod boutiques were earlier in the decade.

Roberts had gained experience of selling on Carnaby Street at Kleptomania, with a mix of exotic clothing and hippie trimmings that had come to be the standard in the area. Mr Freedom was a complete departure, for he realised that what had made earlier boutiques so successful was the shock of the new; a brief and fleeting moment which gave ideas a limited lifespan and meant that constant innovation was vital.

By using a small group of fashion designers including Diane Crawshaw and Dinah Adams, with furniture by Jon Wealleans the reputation of the store soon grew. Shopping became theatre, in this case using subverted Americana, pre-empting the likes of Biba which later exploited Art Deco along similar lines to great commercial success.

Mr Freedom also mirrored the development of Biba when it went on to bigger and better things opening in a large building at 20 Kensington Church Street in 1971, repeating the formula of selling clothes, accessories and furniture together. Prudence Glynn reported in *The Times* the following May that jewellery designed for the store by art college student Ken Leeder in the shape of ice cream cones, iced gems and other edible goodies had sold out almost overnight. 'Sometimes I think that Mr Freedom is less of a shop and more of a mind-reading business, so astute are they at making a haystack-sized boom out of a straw in the fashion wind', she commented.

What had started on the King's Road was now taken to the very extremes of retail design by Jon Wealleans with giant chrome coat hangers, liquorice allsorts cushion covers, even a huge set of teeth as a chair. In the basement was a cafe, Mr Feed'em, with food dyed a selection of comic book colours, all contributing to a giant waking dream of a boutique.

Like so many fashion ventures of the period, the cost of the idea was so great (at somewhere around £35,000 for the interior alone) that the boutique lasted little more than a year, with Trevor Myles returning to retailing on the King's Road and Tommy Roberts opening City Lights Studio in Covent Garden.

'It was totally different, like comic land.'

Tommy Roberts interviewed by Paul Gorman for *The Look* 2006

OPPOSITE PAGE
Twentieth century boys; Marc Bolan
and Mickey Finn pictured in 1971,
T Rex were leaders in glam rock
style and fans of Mr Freedom and
The Hollywood Clothes Shop.
Araldo di Crollalanza/Rex Features

Cobblers to the World

323 King's Road, SW3

OPPOSITE PAGE
Cobblers to the World sold the footwear
fantasies of Terry de Havilland, seen in
the King's Road boutique in 1974.
Mirrorpix

Terry De Havilland, owner and designer of Cobblers to the World was for most of the 1970s the most sought-after cobbler in London. He managed, through a combination of traditional training, wit, daring and a rock star lifestyle, to create some of the most beautiful shoes the fashion world had ever seen, as intoxcating as the fantasy creations emerging from the studios of Bill Gibb, Zandra Rhodes or Ossie Clark.

Trained by his father's firm, Terry Higgins had become Terry de Havilland by the mid-1960s and was soon establishing a reputation selling via manufacturers and retailers such as Ravel and Sacha, as well as supplying smaller boutiques like Susan Locke, also based on the King's Road, and Jonny Moke's business, Rowley and Oram.

Cobblers to the World opened in 1972, a fantasy world of peach mirrors, tented ceilings and velvet covered banquettes where London's rock and film aristocracy came to buy, others to gain inspiration, eventually compromising with something cheaper from their local boutique. Interviewed by *The Independent* in 2009 he described the shop as 'very much party central. We had a machinist in the basement where people came down to have individual shoes made, that was our story anyway.'

In the same way that Mr Freedom challenged with an almost anarchic combination of cultural references, Terry de Havilland shoes became ever more daring, including brightly coloured sequins, snakeskin, even 'Firefly' flashing shoes worked by solar cells, the heels of which lit up every time the wearer's feet left the ground.

The business was incredibly successful, largely because of the brand's unique identity, at one point manufacturing 800 pairs of shoes a week. When Tim Curry needed shoes for his role in *The Rocky Horror Picture Show*, another mix of fashion, fantasy and the bizarre, Cobblers to the World provided them.

The King's Road luxury boutiques were in contrast to the cheap and cheerful atmosphere of Carnaby Street, but both still attracted visitors in huge numbers. *Topfoto*

Big Biba

Big Biba's story in the late 1960s was one of incredible success coupled with incredible design, as Barbara Hulanicki expanded the brand, first with a move to larger premises at 124-126 Kensington High Street in 1969, then to the Derry and Toms department store, creating the brightest star in fashionable London, a magnet for shoppers from across the globe.

Her genius was in the comprehensive nature of the Biba look; she was creating a lifestyle choice rather than a shop, as *The Times* commented on the first Kensington High Street shop in 1971: 'It is an example of unflagging originality in design coupled with a complete logic in the items available'. At the same time as expanding in London, concessions within American department stores were proposed, together with a deal to sell Biba cosmetics in Japan. In both cases Barbara Hulanicki maintained the brand image, commenting in the same year: 'We are not wholesalers and we are not interested in supplying a store buyer's choice from our stock. We say, here's the deal, here's the merchandise'.

Nothing quite prepared the world for her next move – to the massive and redundant Derry & Toms department store – a giant, echoing temple to Art Deco. Big Biba, as it became known, embraced the style and filled it, like some enormous Hollywood film set, with merchandise that made other businesses reel at the sheer size of the operation. Interviewed by the Design Museum in 2007, Barbara Hulanicki recalled: 'There were lots of black and gold signs left and the windows were painted half way up with scratched black paint with gold leaf edges. The woodwork outside was covered in marvellous peeling blue-grey paint. We made long curtains in plum and navy William Morris print with a plum dress fabric lining. I refused to have the flaking woodwork outside painted.'

In the first Kensington High Street Biba it was not uncommon to have around 45,000 people in and out of the 10,000 square feet store on a Saturday. At the height of its popularity Big Biba saw more than a million visitors a week, catapulting the brand from a popular boutique in Kensington to an internationally recognised fashion and tourist attraction, challenging the visitor figures of even Harrods.

Big Biba shoppers certainly got a lot for their money. An early 1970s fashion guide to the capital summarised the situation for its subscribers: 'The layout on the ground floor brings to mind a rather eccentric Art Deco museum; mirrors and palms, marble, and that subdued sepia lighting characteristic of Biba. The Rainbow Room is worth seeing, with its plush, peach cut velvet furnishings and pink mirrors, its cigarette girls in fishnet tights

OPPOSITE PAGE
Full strength glamour courtesy of a 1930s-influenced Biba sequined evening dress for 1969.
Topfoto

OPPOSITE PAGE
Sarah Moon's evocative photographs
for Biba emphasised the changing face
of fashion, with romantic nostalgia
pervading design by the end of the 1960s.
Fashion Museum, Bath.

and bartenders faithfully following the old Savoy cocktail guide. You can't help wondering how many girls are waiting in the same Biba uniform in the same Biba-decorated flats for their dates to come by and take them to dinner there.'

Just as with Tommy Roberts and Mr Freedom, Big Biba combined humour with its hedonistic mix of design references, often playing with the scale of everyday items in displays, like giant baked bean tins in the food hall, even the menswear department had a 'Mistress room' selling exotic underwear. Above all, it was Barbara Hulanicki's vision that bound the whole concept so convincingly together and the fashion press loved it, only occasionally pausing to question the quality of some of the goods bought in the atmospheric subdued lighting and examined in the harsh light of the pavement outside, for that was what Big Biba was all about; theatre. The guide *London on $500 a Day* liked it too recommending 'fringed lampshades, vases of ostrich feathers, high backed peacock wicker chairs, flocked leopard spot wallpaper, a food hall with foot high ice cream sundaes, cosmetic counters with walk round displays that allow you to dip and sample amongst glittering mirrored displays'.

Big Biba's decline was swift, a combination of big business backers tampering with a delicate work of art, and as ever with the economically volatile 1970s, a property crash. Dorothy Perkins had joined forces with Hulanicki and formed Biba Ltd. in 1969, holding a majority share. When this was sold to the British Land Company in 1973, it left the original creators at the mercy of a business partner not versed in the finer points of fashion retailing and Big Biba had closed by 1975.

As remnants of the stock and shop fittings were sold at auction, the seven storey building looked as if had been the scene a giant party which had ended abruptly, leaving the auctioneers to clear up. Many fashion writers at the time pointed out that this was indeed close to the truth, and that it did not bode well for the future of London fashion retailing.

'While others are concentrating on changing their department stores into ill-disguised boutiques, Biba is concentrating on turning their boutique into a well-disguised department store.'

The London Fashion Guide, 1973

Twiggy relaxes in the biggest and best
of the fantasy retailers in 1971. Nothing
compared to the glamour of Big Biba.
Justin de Villeneuve/Getty Images

Zapata

49-51 Old Church Street, sw3

Whether the intention was to accessorise the sleek moss crepe dresses of Ossie Clark, the skilfully-tailored jersey crepe of Jean Muir or the layered fantasy fashion of Bill Gibb, the best designers all bought shoes for their collections from Zapata for one simple reason: Manalo Blahnik.

With little formal training, he managed to match the incredible clothes appearing on the catwalks of early 1970s London with a series of beautifully crafted fantasy creations which defied definition, and sometimes practicality.

He arrived in fashion, and on the London social scene, at a relatively late stage and it was not until 1968 that he re-visited his student days in London after a period in the US; it was *American Vogue* editor Diana Vreeland that first recommended that he concentrated on shoes. Through a combination of good connections and savoir-faire he took London by storm, helped by a definitive collection of shoes for Ossie Clark's catwalk show in 1971, the straps modelled as twisting stems decorated with cherries.

Working almost always alone, he created shoes from the design sketch to completion, at first only selling at Zapata, but taking the opportunity to study both the manufacture and retailing of shoes. With a bank loan and a leap of faith he bought the boutique for £2,000 in 1973 and, like Quorum further along the King's Road, the tiny boutique became a magnet; a latter-day shoe couture salon. In 1974 he became the first man to feature on the cover of *Vogue*, photographed with Angelica Houston by David Bailey, confirming his membership of a very select and internationally recognised group of boutique designer/owners.

As world economies struggled, the suitably blasé 1975 edition of *London on $500 a Day* had no hesitation in directing American visitors to Zapata to be parted from their traveller's cheques, recommending the handmade ladies shoes starting at £75, men's made-to-measure correspondent shoes at £70 and designs in alligator and crocodile from £125. However, unlike many of his contemporaries who failed to survive the economic tumult, Blahnik embraced the tried and tested principals of many couture houses to this day, using headline-grabbing designs as publicity for a core collection of desirable and more affordable designs.

'One of the most exotic spirits in London.'

Women's Wear Daily, 1973

Bus Stop
3 Kensington Church Street, w8
and branches

A popular and successful manufacturing, mail order and boutique chain owned by Lee and Cecil Bender, opening in 1967. Renowned for their reasonably-priced interpretations of high fashion, 40s style tailoring, chic tea dresses, satin jackets and glamorous accessories, the chain later perfected the safari and military looks, opening branches in major British cities together with concessions abroad.

Butler and Wilson
189 Fulham Road, sw7

A temple to costume jewellery founded in the early 1970s by Nicky Butler and Simon Wilson, both of whom shared a love of antique jewellery. Adopting a 'more is more' approach, their glamorous creations took London by storm, satisfying both a nostalgia for Art Nouveau and Art Deco designs, and at the same time selling contemporary pieces in exotic semi-precious stones.

Forbidden Fruit
325 Kings Road, sw3

A tiny boutique selling heavily-embroidered and appliquéd clothing from Afghanistan in the second wave of interest in ethnic dress in the mid 1970s.

The Hollywood Clothes Shop
Hollywood Road, sw10

What Big Biba had started, Johnny Moke continued with the Hollywood Clothes Shop, one part clothing boutique, one part shrine to the golden era of film. Customers for its silky satin and stylish nostalgia included Marc Bolan, who shopped amongst moving displays of classic Hollywood stills and mannequins modelled as stars of the silver screen.

MORE SHOPS

Jeff Banks
27 Duke Street, W1

The designer's first own-label boutique opened in 1975, after success with the Clobber brand, selling affordable glamour; Art Deco prints and nostalgic 1930s and 1940s shapes predominated. Particularly recommended by fashion editors at the time for his long smock shapes and for pretty satin and print separates.

Just Looking
88 Kings Road, SW3

Owned by Harry Finegold and opened in 1967, one of a new generation of luxuriously appointed boutiques on the King's Road, hoping to attract customers who passed by on their way to Quorum.

Susan Locke
312 Kings Road, SW3

A favourite on the King's Road in the late 1960s for being one of the few places selling Terry de Havilland shoes, before he opened his own boutique, together with a selection of Susan Locke designed clothing.

Kensington Market
49 Kensington High Street, W8

Founded in 1969, a maze of 120 tiny stalls selling everything from art to shoes, a breeding ground of talent in the early 1970s, with a host of designers such as Zandra Rhodes at one time running businesses there.

Rowley & Oram
Kensington Market

For a brief period in the early 1970s, the clothes of Mick Oram and John Rowley (later Johnny Moke) attracted the attention of London's fashionable A-list, their stall in Kensington market selling vivid designs in ironic prints, together with some of the most exotic shoe designs of Terry de Havilland.

THIS WAY

Stirling Cooper
26 Wigmore Street, w1 and branches

Established by Jane Whiteside, Geoffrey Cooper and Ronald Stirling as a wholesale ready-to-wear company, Stirling Cooper opened a boutique on Wigmore Street as a 'testing ground' in 1969, employing 24 year old Antony Price as one of a small group of in-house designers. The great success of Stirling Cooper was its pricing structure, and by bringing a little of the glamour of the more expensive boutiques to its customers, the chain was able to eventually expand nationwide. In 1970 coats were around £9, with dresses designed by Antony Price at £8.10s.

Stop the Shop
126 King's Road, sw3

Opened in 1969 and part of the boutique empire of Harry Finegold, it was famed for its gradually revolving central floor designed by Garnett, Cloughley and Blakemore. Customers moved, the stock did not, and there was a humorous editorial in the fashion press at the time on the possible consequences of mechanical malfunction.

EVEN MORE

By the late 1960s the King's Road had developed a run of distinctively designed luxury boutiques opposite the Duke of York's Headquarters, including Harry Finegold's Just Looking.
Alan Messer/Rex Features

By the early 1970s London was used to boutiques, which in effect pulled the rug out from under many who relied solely on the shock of the new to sell.

Carnaby Street had not been taken seriously by the majority of style commentators since the mid-1960s, but had fought on, witnessing the comings and goings of boutiques and souvenir shops. As Hardy Clarke in the *Daily Express* claimed, the street was 'tottering towards the end of its 10 year run of success'. He blamed the retailers themselves, claiming that the service, courtesy and facilities were inadequate, but even if this were the case, a much wider and gloomier economic picture dictated that there was less money to spend on non-essentials than in the boom years of the previous decade.

In 1973 Westminster Council had spent £60,000 on refurbishments including the much derided multi-coloured rubber paving which effectively cancelled out any actual improvements by making the area look something like the set of *The Wizard of Oz*. It was at this time that a number of established retailers in the street began to run at a loss, most notably the John Stephen empire; its terrific run of success was over by 1974 when it slipped into the red, eventually being sold in 1976.

A similar picture developed on the other side of town, confirming that the rules had changed for even the greatest pioneers of London's boutique movement. Biba was by then owned with a majority share by British Land who forced the closure of Barbara Hulanicki's inspirational venture on Kensington High Street in 1975, bringing to an end a decade of success in the area.

These high profile closures were by no means restricted to the boutiques, with the couture and ready-to-wear businesses of the likes of Bill Gibb, Ossie Clark and many others slipping in and out of receivership and bankruptcy, sometimes re-emerging for another attempt with a new backer. What had changed for good was the perception that opening a boutique was easy, and that with a little luck and design knowledge, success was guaranteed, which had certainly appeared the case for a period in the early 1960s.

Economic deterioration often brings with it a polarisation in politics and fashion, creating a culture of extremes. London's boutique scene in the first half of 1970s had developed two schools of thought.

The first had brought Big Biba and Mr Freedom, the second started with Vivienne Westwood and Malcolm McLaren and was to dominate fashion innovation, boutique retailing and perceptions of taste in the capital for the remainder of the decade.

OPPOSITE PAGE
In 1973 Westminster council had
spent £60,000 on a much derided
multi-coloured paving scheme in
Carnaby Street, effectively ending
the street's credibility as the centre
of fashionable London.
Robert Taylor/Rex Features

Paradise Garage
Let it Rock
Too Fast to Live,
Too Young to Die
SEX
Seditionaries –
Clothes for Heroes
430 King's Road, sw3

Boutique retailing in the 1970s is inextricably linked to 430 King's Road and in turn to Vivienne Westwood and Malcolm McLaren. It was their rapidly evolving vision of fashion and confrontational marketing that wedded clothing to politics and music as never before and created in a permanent location an intense creative flux, until then only experienced in the densely packed stalls of Kensington Market or Camden Town.

After returning to the King's Road from Mr Freedom in 1971 Trevor Myles launched Paradise Garage. Using a formula which had worked well in the past, he commissioned the Electric Colour Co. to create a fantasy environment that matched the merchandise, in this case a mixture of second-hand and new denim, screen printed t-shirts and a heady mix of vaguely 1950s Americana. With it came the attention-grabbing trimmings including a petrol pump outside, the exterior looking like a slice of New Orleans – part fashion market, part Louisiana bar.

Vivienne Westwood's association with the shop started when Malcolm McClaren, along with his friend Patrick Casey, leased a small amount of space from Myles at the back of Paradise Garage, using her to design clothing and opening the entire shop as Let it Rock in 1971. A mixture of old and new Teddy Boy clothes, ephemera and in part a 1950s devotees social club, it flew in the face of mainstream fashion but developed a devoted following. By selling re-made clothing amongst the vintage, Vivienne Westwood started a manufacturing business which is still operating in the same location today; it was the first of a rapid succession of incarnations.

In 1972 the shop became Too Fast To Live, Too Young to Die, accurately summarising the hedonistic edge of the pair, for this was no normal fashion partnership. Developing and subverting the Edwardian clothes of the Teddy Boys, they continued with a mix of old and new before a departure into the uncharted waters of bondage and fetish fashion with SEX in 1974, selling clothes and accessories in rubber and leather in the heart of Chelsea, a pre-meditated and provocative move.

This was new ground in British retailing; very different to the fantasy interiors of the boutiques which had caused so much attention a few years previously, but arguably designed to generate the same outcome: publicity. In a largely residential area, used to the high jinks of boutique owners, SEX was seen as one taboo too far and in 1975 it was prosecuted for 'exposing to public view an indecent exhibition'.

The pair became synonymous with Punk and it was 430 Kings Road that provided the style, whatever the particular

OPPOSITE PAGE
Same address, different shop; SEX was one of many anarchic incarnations of 430 King's Road and opened in 1974 selling a mix of bondage gear, leather and punk fashion.
Sheila Rock/Rex Features

Sales assistant Jordan inside SEX, essentially a traditional boutique but with an anti-establishment credo, an old swing ticket from Let it Rock is still in use.
Sheila Rock/Rex Features

name of the boutique that year. The clothes were deconstructed, overtly sexual, deliberately provocative and courted controversy as standard. Another change of name to Seditionaries – Clothes for Heroes came in 1976, as in time did bondage trousers and t-shirts with printed legends and images calculated to offend. One of these, called 'Two Naked Cowboys', challenged British censorship on a number of levels: nudity, homosexuality, freedom of speech, taste and decency – all on one printed cotton shirt. McLaren's Sex Pistols were the clothes personified, with both working to promote the other, in effect a very modern marriage of fashion, fetish and fame.

Like all designers of note, Westwood realised that nothing invoked attention like a complete change of course, so as Punks thronged the King's Road, photographed by the tourists and celebrated on postcards, she moved on to New Romanticism, already anticipating and influencing the fashion of the following decade.

Acme Attractions
153 Kings Road, SW3

Owned by John Krevine and Steph Raynor and originally located in the basement of Antiquarius, Acme Attractions sold juke boxes, vintage clothing and shoes. Mixing the sharpest styles from the preceding 30 years, it attracted a cosmopolitan following, acting as one of the new social centres of the King's Road. In 1977 a move to 153 King's Road and a change of name to BOY saw the boutique competing directly with Seditionaries at World's End, selling cheaper versions of bondage and punk-influenced fashion. The brand continued into the 1980s, selling body-conscious club wear in branches on the King's Road and in Soho.

City Lights
54 Shorts Gardens, WC2

In late 1972, after the demise of Mr Freedom, Tommy Roberts moved his ideas on to Covent Garden, which was at that time just beginning to become popular as a retail location. Selling a mix of clothing, shoes, handmade hats and cleverly designed perspex jewellery, he continued the tradition of the 'one stop' boutique, also offering a mail order service.

MORE SHOPS

Ten:
The End of the Road

Choosing at what point to draw *Boutique London* to a close was as emotive a decision as deciding which was the first, or last, or greatest of the capital's boutiques.

Certainly the story of both Carnaby Street and the King's Road is definable in terms of who did what where and when, but the wider fashion landscape of the capital has always been much more ambiguous, with very different approaches often running in parallel until one becomes prevalent.

At the same time as Vivienne Westwood and Malcolm McLaren were setting out to scandalise, some of the capital's most beautiful couture clothing to date was being created by Bill Gibb, Yuki and Zandra Rhodes to international acclaim. In reality the publicity stunts at 430 King's Road were building the foundations of an international fashion brand, particularly ironic given its origins in anarchic slogans and court cases.

What was clear by the mid-1970s, was that fashion retailing had essentially polarised and that the large number of individual boutiques which opened in the preceding 15 years would certainly not be replaced in the same way, with retail chains and centralisation becoming familiar themes.

Paul Smith, Antony Price, Red or Dead, Bodymap and Pam Hogg all continued the tradition of the boutique into the 1980s and to some extent Camden Market and Hyper Hyper nurtured new talent in the same way as the first small boutiques of Carnaby Street. What London lost, then, was the democracy of the boutique; the idea that it was possible to strike out and run a fashion business relatively centrally and cheaply without life-changing consequences if it failed.

So, to future boutique pioneers and risk-takers this book is dedicated.

Teenagers outside BOY on the King's
Road in 1979: shops continued to
open, selling the latest style, but the
glory days of boutique retailing had
drawn to a close.
Janette Beckman/Getty Images

BIBLIOGRAPHY, THANKS & INDEX

Bibliography

Richard Barnes, *Mods!*, Plexus Publishing, 2009

Christopher Breward, Edwina Ehrman, Caroline Evans, *The London Look: Fashion From Street to Catwalk*, Museum of London, 2004

Christopher Breward, David Gilbert, Jenny Lister, *Swinging Sixties*, V&A Publishing, 2006

Ernestine Carter, *With Tongue in Chic*, Michael Joseph, 1974

Nic Cohn, *Today there are No Gentleman*, Weidenfeld & Nicolson, 1971

Max Décharné, *King's Road: The Rise and Fall of the Hippest Street in the World*, Weidenfeld & Nicolson, 2005

Amy De la Haye, *The Cutting Edge: 50 Years of British Fashion 1947–1997*, V&A Publishing 1996

Marnie Fogg, *Boutique: A '60s Cultural Phenomenon*, Octopus, 2003

Paul Gorman, *The Look: Adventures in Pop and Rock Fashion*, Sanctuary Publishing, 2001

Barbara Hulanicki, *From A to Biba*, Hutchinson, 1983

Janey Ironside, *Janey: An Autobiography*, Michael Joseph, 1973

Ferne Kadish and Kathleen Kirtland, *London on $500 a Day*, Collier Books, 1975

Farrol Kahn Ltd, *The London Fashion Guide*, Spring 1975

Shawn Levy, *Ready Steady Go!: The Smashing Rise and Giddy Fall of Swinging London*, Fourth Estate, 2003

Alwyn Turner, *The Biba Experience*, Antique Collectors Club, 2004

Mary Quant, *Quant on Quant*, Cassell, 1966

Judith Watt, *Ossie Clark 1965–74*, V&A Publishing, 2003

Online resources:
www.vintage-a-peel.co.uk
www.kerrytaylorauctions.com
www.vam.ac.uk
www.fashionmuseum.co.uk

Acknowledgements

With thanks to James Smith, Matthew Freedman, Alison Hart and Anna Morton at ACC, Rosemary Harden, Elaine Uttley and all at the Fashion Museum in Bath, Robert Shaw at Northbank, Malcolm English, Kerry Taylor, Liz Eggleston at Vintage-a-Peel, Colin and Sonia Butler, Megan and Natasha Lester and with especial thanks to Geoff Cox.